EARTH QUEST

The aim of the *Earth Quest* series is to examine and explain how shamanic principles can be applied in the journey towards self-discovery – and beyond.

Each person's Earth quest is the search for meaning and purpose in their life – it is the establishment of identity and the realization of inner potentials and individual responsibility.

Each book in the series examines aspects of a life science that is in harmony with the Earth and shows how each person can attune themselves to nature. Each book imparts knowledge of the Craft of Life.

John Matthews is an authority on Arthurian and Celtic traditions and has over 40 books in print on these and other themes, including *The Elements of the Arthurian Tradition, The Little Book of Arthurian Wisdom, The Celtic Shaman* and *The Celtic Shaman's Pack*. He has taught classes on Celtic Shamanism and Arthurian myths, is active in the promotion of the growing story-teller's movement and much in demand internationally as a speaker at conferences on myth and story. He is married to the writer Caitlín Matthews, with whom he has collaborated on numerous books, including *The Encyclopaedia of Celtic Wisdom*.

Healing the Wounded King

Soul Work and the Quest for the Grail

JOHN MATTHEWS

ELEMENT

Shaftesbury, Dorset • Rockport, Massachusetts • Brisbane, Queensland

© Element Books Limited 1997
Text © John Matthews 1997

First published in Great Britain in 1997 by
Element Books Limited
Shaftesbury, Dorset SP7 8BP

Published in the USA in 1997 by
Element Books, Inc
PO Box 830, Rockport, MA 01966

Published in Australia in 1997 by
Element Books Limited
for Jacaranda Wiley Limited
33 Park Road, Milton, Brisbane 4064

Illustrations by Anthea Helliwell
Cover design by Max Fairbrother
Design by Roger Lightfoot
Typeset by Footnote Graphics, Warminster, Wilts
Printed and bound in Great Britain by
J W Arrowsmiths, Bristol

British Library Cataloguing in Publication
data available

Library of Congress Cataloging in Publication
data available

ISBN 1-85230-955-5

Contents

DEDICATION

To Emrys who may find this useful one day
And to David and Julie for making a stranger welcome in
another land.

To make the sick knight thrive,
A herb to cure all pain
That in a hedge had lain
He spied, and thence he plucked it.

The Rig Veda

The Ancestors, I ask them,
What came first?
The hurt or the hurter?
The bowman or the quarry?
Who hunts who
Down what chasms of time?
How do we heal
The ancient hurts
That make us wasteland?
How raise up the children
Of the lesser dead?

Where Does the Wasteland Start?
Caitlín Matthews

Foreword

INJURIES, WOUNDS AND HEALING

You are about to read a remarkable and very helpful book. Through John Matthews' depth of scholarship and intuitive insights, the ancient story of the Grail and the Wounded King is shown to contain elements of universal and timeless wisdom and power pertinent to modern humanity. We discover that the images contained within this story are not just the fanciful imaginings of medieval and pre-medieval story-tellers; in fact we discover, as John and those with whom he worked discovered, that these images are really portals into a reservoir of healing energy that can bring us wholeness and restoration in the midst of suffering. Though the story is ancient, the healing power is contemporary and present. This is a true gift from our ancestors.

The wisdom and healing in this story comes from understanding the nature of wounds and woundedness. This is timely, for we live in an age that seems particularly obsessed with being wounded. It seems that the slightest affront to our personal sensibilities is taken as a wound, and television talk shows parade bizarre examples of dysfunctional lives in a subtext that suggests all of us are psychologically wounded in some way.

Likewise, we are told by the authors of popular self-help books that we are all wounded, that we all come from dysfunctional families, and that everything that happened to us when we were children creates a wound in our psyches. In such a context, we may well become confused over what a wound is and the difference between injuries and wounds. We can turn every hurt into a personal waste land that resists healing.

Perhaps part of the healing power in the Arthurian tales of the Grail and the Wounded King lies simply in reminding us what a wound is and what it is not. Throughout these stories, people are constantly being injured. They are cut by swords, impaled by spears, bashed with maces, and hacked at with axes, and those who are not killed outright heal and go forth to engage in new encounters.

But the Fisher King is different. He is injured, but he is not called the Injured King; he is called the Wounded King. He has an injury that not only will not heal, but which also has an effect beyond his own personal well-being. For with this injury, the land itself becomes wounded and turns into a waste land. A generative, vital power is lost.

Obviously, this is no ordinary injury. An injury is something that heals. It may be painful, it may be debilitating, but it can heal; life goes on. Furthermore, an injury is personal, and the healing is personal. Though medical help may assist and augment the healing process, ultimately it is the body's own regenerative power that effects healing.

We all have injuries in our lives, and we can all move on from them, however painful they might have been. An injury has a beginning and an ending; we move past the trauma, the scars, the memories, and get on with our lives.

However, a wound as presented in the story of the Fisher King has no closure. It remains open. It becomes the defining element of the person, pulling one's identity into itself. The king is not a king who has been injured and is recovering; he is the Wounded King. That is his identity, an identity of loss and disempowerment.

Furthermore, a wound is meta-personal. The injury was inflicted on the king, but the wound affects all the kingdom, because of the mystical connection between the king and the land. An injury may affect our personal bodies, emotions, or mental states, but a wound affects our connections and relation-ships. It affects how we creatively participate in the universe by drawing our creative energy and attention into itself.

Anyone who has worked therapeutically with people knows that there are individuals who are deeply wounded by life, but whose wounds do not heal because they participate in its continuance. The original injury may have been caused by another, but the wound continues to be self-inflicted. The wound has become part of their identities in ways that make its healing more fearful than the suffering it brings, so they discover ways to maintain it. Living with the wound is safer than taking the steps back into a process of creative participation and engagement with the world that will heal it, but will transform the identity in the process. Better the waste land which is familiar than a verdant, abundant land that brings a multiplicity of new lies and demands.

In short, a wound may come into being when we use an injury to separate ourselves from life and from the creative, participatory responsibilities that come with it. A wound may come when we use injury as a basis for self-definition. Or a wound may come when the inner, spiritual connective tissue that links us with the rest of creation is damaged in a way that leaves us feeling cut off and disempowered.

However the wound comes, the story is clear on how it is healed. The Grail restores health and wholeness to the King and hence to the Land. But what is the Grail but a primordial symbol of participatory engagement with a larger wholeness? It is the restoration of connectedness and the responsibility that comes with it.

To discover the Grail and to bring its healing power to the Wounded King, Perceval must ask a question, which is an act of going beyond oneself to connect with a larger world. A question is a vulnerability, an admission of a lack of knowledge; in its openness, it is almost like a wound in itself. It is an act of extending oneself into an unknown territory. It is an act of connection.

When Perceval first comes to the Grail Castle, he is self-contained. Shyness constrains him. He does not ask the question, even though he sees wonders manifest before him. He does not make himself vulnerable. So the Grail is not revealed, and he goes away, his mission unfulfilled. It is only when he comes back and with greater humility and wisdom asks his question that the connection is made and healing can take place. Healing comes from going beyond the personal self into participation in a larger wholeness that is both supportive and demanding. It comes when we begin to take responsibility for more than just ourselves.

Of course, the story of the Wounded King and the Grail can be interpreted in many ways. The wonder and power of John Matthews' work in this book is that he goes beyond interpretation to show us that in the images themselves and how we take them into ourselves lies an experience of connectedness with the deep powers of wholeness, creativity, and healing in our world, as well as in ourselves. He has performed a wonderful service and given us all a gift.

Reading this book is like entering the Grail Castle itself. In it we may find the questions that connect us, the Grail that heals us and the kingship that allows us to bring new life to a world sorely in need of it.

DAVID SPANGLER, 1996

Preface

This book is about woundedness. It is also about healing. It is based on the premise that we are all, men and women, living at the end of the 20th century, wounded in some way – physically, psychically, spiritually, or in all three ways. It also assumes that we wish to heal these wounds, and it offers a way of doing so, using the Arthurian myths relating to the Grail, that has been successfully tried and tested over a number of years and with a wide variety of people.

My work with this ancient method of healing our wounded nature began in 1990 when I was in the USA, teaching and visiting with friends. One day I received a visit from someone who had recently suffered a painful loss, and who felt utterly unable to cope with life. He asked me if I could suggest anything that might help. As I pondered this question, there came, unbidden into my mind, the thought: Tell him to meditate on the story of the 'Wounded King'. This story, which will be examined in detail in Chapter 2, concerns a quest undertaken by a youth named Perceval, to discover a magical vessel of healing and plenty, and in the process of this search to heal the mysterious Fisher King of a wound which has resisted all attempts to find a cure, and which causes the land over which he rules to become desolate. The healing finally takes place through the asking of a question, which sets in motion not only the healing of the king, but also of the land.

I gave my friend a brief rendition of this story, which is an important part of the myth of the Grail, and suggested he go home and spend some time with the images and thoughts that arose from its contemplation. I heard nothing more for several days, but then I received an ecstatic phone call. 'I don't know where that story comes from, but it's changed me forever. I feel I can cope again. Thank you!'

A few days after this another person, this time a woman who had taken part in one of my workshops, came to me and related how she had just ended a long-term relationship, and was so hurt by this that she felt as though her life was over. Again, was there anything I could do to help? After a moment's reflection I referred her to the story of the Wounded King, and suggested that she meditate on it. A few weeks later, on my return to England, I received a letter from her in which she said that she felt greatly restored by the story and that meditating upon it had revealed all kinds of insights into her personal life situation which she had simply not been able to see before.

By this time I was feeling excited. I had always known that the story was a powerful one, but I had not realized that meditating on it could bring about such a vital transformation. I began to think of ways to focus and extend the work with the story, and invited a number of colleagues to work with me. We were all astonished at the powerful and positive results we attained together and as a result of this, in 1992, I began to do a number of experimental workshops, with limited numbers and by invitation only, based around the story of the Wounded King. In addition, I now included other parts of the Grail story, including a second important tale, 'The Damsels of the Wells' since it had become obvious that these stories related just as much to women as to men. The results were remarkable, and I found that there were many different ways of working with these stories, and their imagery, in a healing and nurturing way. Finally in 1994 I did a full-scale open workshop during a conference on the Western Mysteries at the Findhorn Foundation in Scotland, and began to send out a questionnaire to selected people who had worked with me in the past. (See Appendix 2.)

The result is this book, which I would not have been able to write without the participation of friends, colleagues and workshop participants both in England and the USA. To all of those who volunteered to explore this work, I owe a great debt of gratitude.

To others I owe a more specific debt. Among those are David Spangler, with whom I took the first tentative steps towards understanding the Wounded King with new eyes, and who read and commented upon the first version of this manuscript.

Janet Piedelato, who is one of the finest healers I know, and who has not only taught me a great deal by example, but who also came to my aid at a crucial period in the writing when I began to suffer the wounds of the Grail within myself; and Gareth Knight, for the week we spent together in 1995 teaching the mysteries of the Grail, during which time I learned many valuable things. Finally, to my wife Caitlín, whose own ongoing work has so much to do with the kind of healing I am trying to access here, and which is so polarized. Also for her work on the *Mabinogion*, which she has so wonderfully shared with me over the years, and for the support she gave me during a difficult few weeks in July 1996.

But perhaps the greatest debt of all is to the voice that whispered in my ear, six years ago, 'Tell him to meditate on the Wounded King!'

JOHN MATTHEWS
Oxford, 1996

The Exercises

Notes on the Exercises

There are two primary methods of working, described in this book: guided vizualization and shamanic journey. The following note is intended to offer general guidelines in these techniques.

1 Guided Visualization

There are a number of ways to do this. One is to read the text of the visualization aloud onto a tape and then play it back to yourself when you can be sure of a quiet time without interruption. Another is to listen to the text on the pre-recorded tape which accompanies this book (details of where and how to order will be found in the resources section at the end of this book). The essential requirement is to be able to sit somewhere peaceful and quiet (preferably in an upright chair to prevent falling asleep) where you will not be disturbed, and to give yourself up to the imagery of the visualization. Try to be there, in the scene, as much as possible. Try not to see the whole thing on a TV screen in your head; the more you are present in the visualization the more you will get out of it. When you are done, give yourself time to return to normal consciousness, and write down any messages or other reactions you may have experienced while meditating. If you feel at all shaken or disturbed by the experience – a not unusual reaction given the power of the imagery and the depths of our woundedness – fix yourself a hot drink and have something to eat. This will help ground you again, and allow the effects of the visualization to settle.

2 SHAMANIC JOURNEYING

When you take a shamanic journey you leave your everyday consciousness and enter the realm of subtle reality which is generally referred to throughout this book as the Otherworld. Within this timeless dimension you will be journeying, accompanied by an inner-world helper, to one of three realms: Upperworld, Middleworld or Underworld. These are accessed by entering a light trance, induced by listening to a rhythmic sound-source, such as a drum or a plucked string. A number of pre-recorded tapes to enable journeying are currently available and will be found listed in the resource section at the end of this book. Do not worry that you will be put into a trance from which you cannot wake: all the recommended tapes have a call-back signal on them, which returns you naturally and easily to your everyday consciousness.

From time to time you will almost certainly experience things which are disturbing to you. The nature of the work makes this inevitable. Generally, these are entirely beneficial, and should be worked with accordingly. However, should you at any time encounter things which are particularly distressing, you can return from your journey at will by bringing yourself back to your usual state of consciousness. In most instances you remain fully aware of your physical surroundings, but simply drift off, rather as in a daydream, but with greater control over where you go and what you experience. Unlike the visualization technique, where you are following a guided description of events, the journey takes you where you personally need to go, or where your spirit helpers need to take you to find the answers you are seeking.

To begin a journey you need to lie full length on the floor or on a bed (taking care not to be too comfortable in case sleep is induced). Then, cover your eyes with a scarf to shut out the light and, relaxing as much as you can, put on the sound tape (headphones are advisable as this helps to exclude distracting noises) and listen to the drumming. Go with the sound, listening not to the beat itself, but rather to the resonance, the carrier wave of sound which will help you to shift into another mode of consciousness. Again, once you have completed the journey, you should record your experiences and make a good strong cup of tea or coffee to earth yourself. If you find it difficult to remember what you experienced, or indeed to see anything, try journeying aloud, recording your experiences into a second tape-recorder. The action of vocalizing the journey helps trigger the mind's ability to 'see', and you will also have a complete and reliable record of your experiences. Additional information on the nature of this work will be found on pp13–16.

Introduction

As Robert Bly has pointed out, while the bird stores its instinctive knowledge in its brain, humanity has stored its innate wisdom in myth, legend and story (18). One of the primary mythic story cycles of the West, and a rich source of native wisdom, is the Matter of Arthur and his Knights, which concerns itself with their trials and adventures, with the great quest for the Holy Grail, and with their attempt to re-create a perfect earthly realm. One of the key components of this mythology concerns the Wounded King, a mysterious monarch who possesses a terrible wound that will not heal until a certain set of circumstances exists. Among these is the coming of a 'foolish' person who will ask a particular question, setting in motion a chain reaction which results not only in the healing of the King, but also of the land over which he rules and which is itself mysteriously wounded and remains wasted and dead.

In this book the Wounded King is seen as a representative of everyone who is wounded, and who has lost, or forgotten, the ability to restore him- or herself to health. (It is important to note here that this story applies just as powerfully to women as to men.) It relates mythical stories to human feelings and situations, finding within these tales much that illuminates our own state of being, and which teaches us to look at life through new eyes. It is based on more than twenty years of work with the Arthurian stories and, more recently, on work of a practical kind with people who were wounded and who have sought healing through the power of myth.

The ideas contained here are concerned primarily with the

soul's journey, which everyone takes and which leads each of us to somewhere different but which yet, in the end, leads us all to the same place! In this book you will hear a good deal about the shaman's journey, which is like the journey of the soul in that it is essentially a quest for wholeness. It is this wholeness which promises health and a sense of connection to a larger world which is an ideal we all carry in our hearts. 'Come with me on a journey,' says the story-teller, 'into wonderful lands both rich and strange, where wonders abound and miracles happen every day.' You are invited to set out on such a journey, following in the steps of those who have surveyed the way ahead and left signposts for us to follow. The story we are going to explore is just one set of signposts: many others exist to be discovered and explored in time. Our journey leads us in search of the miraculous – of healing and restoration – of the kingdom of the Grail and the Water of Life.

The healing gift of story is something we tend to overlook nowadays. Yet story has the power to heal a remarkable number of hurts. It can, literally, enchant us, help us to discover the truth about ourselves, find new strengths, lay old ghosts. The story of the Grail is perhaps the single greatest healing story of all, and by working with it in a deeply personal way, we open ourselves to its many levels, where we will find, again and again, our own situations and problems reflected back with the ever-present opportunity to make changes for the better. Thus a simple story can and does bring healing to the individual, restoring within us a sense of completeness and connectedness that is deeply absent from our inner being, making us restless and wounding us more deeply than we know.

One of the latest and most glorious manifestations of this particular myth – and one that has everything to do with our own quest for healing – is the 1991 motion picture *The Fisher King*, written by Richard La Gravenese and directed by Terry Gilliam. This is a modern re-telling of the quest for the Grail, which touches upon the very core of the Wounded King story.

The setting is New York, where we are introduced to Jack Lucas, a radio talk-show host with a line in deadpan, down-beat chat. In the novelization of the movie-script he is described as personifying 'You Are What You Own, Wear, Drive, Eat, You Are Where You Live, You Are Who You Sleep With' and – most important of all – Jack was a man whose own success he happily measured by the failure of others (21). One evening he goes too

far, goading a disturbed individual to take action against the
yuppies and up-town well-healed people who he perceives as
mocking him. The man's response is to take a shot-gun and,
walking into an up-town restaurant, start blasting away. In the
resulting carnage a gentle professor of medieval history sees his
young wife shot to death, while he escapes without a mark. The
resulting feeling of horror and guilt drives him over the edge
into madness, in which he assumes the character of the street-
bum 'Parry', a name derived from Perceval. Here he lives out a
fantasy life based around the story of the Grail, building a kind
of shrine in a basement boiler-room, seldom going out for fear of
a terrible figure that only he sees, whom he calls the Red Knight.

Lucas, meanwhile, has lost his job at the radio station and
turned to drink, wracked with guilt over the effect of his casual
words, and the failure of his own life. One night he is set upon
by a group of thugs, and is rescued by Parry, who takes him
back to his shelter. Gradually the two men strike up a strange
relationship, and bit by bit Lucas learns the true identity of his
friend. Finally, in a dramatic climax, Parry is himself beaten
almost to death. As he lies in a coma in hospital, Lucas sets out
on a quest for the Grail, which Parry believes to be in the
medieval-style pent-house belonging to a millionaire. Lucas
scales the sheer walls of the 'castle' and steals the 'Grail' – in
reality a commemorative cup presented to the millionaire in his
youth. In the process he saves the vessel's owner, who has been
affected by a stroke, but who is saved when Lucas sets off the
alarm.

Escaping with the stolen cup, Jack takes it to Parry's bedside
and places it between the hands of the unconscious man. Gradually Parry returns to consciousness, barely aware of anything
save the object between his hands, 'something cold, heavy,
metal, silver . . . he felt it, touching it all over. Looking down,
Parry saw with an enormous surge of joy what it was he was
holding. It was the Holy Grail, the only thing that could cure
his incurable wound'. (21)

Parry makes a full recovery, remembering and accepting his
wife's death, and forgiving Lucas for his part in it. The Grail has
cured both men, transforming their wounds into strengths. It is
healing power of this kind which is at the heart of this book,
and which we shall be searching for throughout our journey.
But first we need to know something about the nature of our
wounds and the effects they have on our lives, and to do this

we need to ask ourselves questions. Just as the central healing reflex of the Grail myth is the asking of the ritual question 'Whom does the Grail serve?', so we need to go through the process of identifying the problems which we should be addressing. This does not mean listing every single wound you can think of, or dwelling upon them unnecessarily. It is simply a means of accessing some of the problems you will be working with as you proceed through the book.

Thus you might begin by asking: 'Where am I wounded, vulnerable, in pain, hurting? What caused this? Did something leave, enter, or get lost in me at that time? What memories of that time do I bear now? Where can I go for help?' Questions such as these begin to open up the whole question of wounded-ness, and prepare the way for healing.

It is important to keep in mind that the objective in working with these problems is to seek healing for them, and that by owning your wounds you are not giving them power over you or dwelling upon them in an unhealthy way. Rather, you are submitting them to the light of the Grail, which has more than enough power to heal them.

The effect of the Grail on those who come into its presence has always been remarkable. In the 15th century *Le Morte Darthur* of Sir Thomas Malory, the first coming of the wondrous vessel to Camelot is unforgettably described.

> *Then they heard the cracking and crying of thunder, so that they thought all the place should be destroyed. And in the midst of this blast entered a sunbeam seven times more clear than daylight ever was. . . Then began every knight to behold each other, and all saw each other as seeming more fair than ever before. And there was no knight that might speak for a while, but they looked at each other as though they were dumb. Then there entered into the hall the Holy Grail covered with white samite, but no one might see it clearly, nor who carried it. And here was all the hall filled with good odours, and every knight had such meets and drinks as he best loved in all the world. (12)*

In our own time this perception has changed but little, as we can see in this passage from a modern Grail work, *The Great Return* by Arthur Machen (Penguin Books, 1946):

> *. . .if there be paradise in meat and drink, so much the more is there par-adise in the scent of the green leaves at evening and in the appearance of the sea and in the redness of the sky: and . . . [in] . . . a certain vision of a real world about us all the while, of a language that was only secret because we would not take the trouble to listen to it and to discern it.*

In the presence of the Grail:

> *Old men felt young again, eyes that had been growing dim now saw clearly, and saw a world that was like paradise, the same world, it is true, but a world rectified and glowing, as if an inner flame shone in all things, and behind all things. (ibid)*

It is to this inner flame, this blazing and glorious light, that we take our wounds to be healed, tracing the outlines of the Grail story within us, recognizing the true nature of the world around us, and perceiving with new eyes the patterns of woundedness and the promise of healing held out to us by this wondrous tale.

1   The Wounded Soul

I am ill because of wounds to the soul...

Healing D H Lawrence

THE NATURE OF THE WOUND

Working with different states of woundedness requires that we make certain definitions before we begin. The kind of wounds referred to in this book are not so much physical as spiritual. They can take many forms, and not all of them will respond to the kinds of healing discussed below, which are themselves essentially spiritual by nature. Ultimately all these wounds derive from an inner state, from the health or otherwise of the soul, though they can manifest themselves physically, psychically or spiritually. They may be purely personal, or they may extend to include our direct family, our friends, and finally our whole race! They may blight a relationship, ruin a good day out, wreck our chances of getting a good job, or systematically erode our inner lives until we feel empty and useless.

Common indications of woundedness manifest in characteristics with which many of us will be familiar. These can be grouped roughly into 'active' and 'passive' qualities:

Active	Passive
Anger	Loss of vitality
Self-pity	Fear of failure
Aggression	Inadequacy
Self-aggrandisement	Emptiness
Combativeness	Detachment
Cynicism	Helplessness
Manipulation	Lack of love
Repression	Lack of encouragement

Most of you will recognize these qualities within your own lives. How many times have you become furiously angry over the most insignificant thing? Or felt filled with self-pity, rejection, or helplessness when faced with a difficult problem? Who has not, at some time or other, felt inadequate, or empty, and turned to cynicism, or aggression, or self-aggrandisement to disguise the truth? Have we not all suffered from lack of love, or encouragement, when we most needed it?

These are only some of the most immediately recognizable forms that our wounds can take. We can also be wounded by gender, age, race, culture and religion, in fact by the human condition itself, which fosters so many kinds of wounds, and which provides us with endless role models to live up to, but seldom if ever offers a cure for the desolation of spirit which can attack us at any moment. All these things hurt us at a very deep level, at a soul level, and they all leave scars within us.

Many of the people who answered the questionnaire expressed the presence of these, and other, characteristics, either at some specific point in their lives, or constantly. A book could probably be written on each of these states, but the important thing to recognize is that all, without exception, either lead to or derive from a state of *unconnectedness*, an inability to create or to progress forward through life, to connect with either our immediate surroundings or with other people.

If you have ever stood in front of a great work of art, listened to a great musical work, read a mighty and noble book, or watched a deeply moving play or motion picture, and felt utterly unmoved, un-shaken, detached, this is an expression of the wound. If you think you possess everything to make you happy: a big house, a car, as many possessions as you want, a happy and loving family, and yet still feel empty inside, this is another. Equally, if you feel that everything is too much for you, that life is overwhelming you at every point or that, as one correspondent shared, you have only 'two reactions to any new challenge – anger or despair', then you too are suffering. Of course, there are many other manifestations of woundedness, but most stem from the basic type.

Once people turned to religion for an answer, and in some cases we can still find solutions there. But for many people the disciplines and requirements of following a prescribed religious way of life are too stringent, or fail to satisfy. This is itself a symptom of our wounded state. Many of us recognize that none of these answers are enough. We experience a kind of inner hunger which nothing will assuage. Sometimes we are driven to do foolish things to cover the pain we cannot express: we may spend money unnecessarily on new things, buy bigger and better TVs or cars, or spend all our time lost in the fantasy world of TV and movies. Or else we turn to drink or drugs and lose ourselves in a world where everything is invested with false meaning.

But none of this will do. Emptiness persists, and nothing can fill the blank space. We may become angry, and those around us and nearest to us can suffer as a result. But still our feeling of emptiness increases, and our anger grows with it. We become more and more desperate, less and less able to function as complete human beings.

THE WOUNDED HEALER

It is at this point (if we are fortunate) that the Healer appears. He or she is usually someone who has suffered the same wounds as ourselves. He or she offers both wisdom and healing, often of a startling and challenging kind, urging us to question our state of being.

In many cultures this kind of work was the task of the shaman, who was sometimes called 'the Wounded Healer'. Shamans were the first doctors, the first psychiatrists, the first priests. Their skills date back to the oldest records of human existence. Shamanism works directly in the realm of the soul, and as such it offers a particularly powerful way of treating the innate causes of woundedness. In recent times shamanism has become almost as widespread as it was long ago; teachers and practitioners have sprung up throughout the West and have begun to instruct people in the techniques of inner journey work and co-operation with the spirits. At the same time they have begun to re-educate people into the mysteries of the land, which itself contains the potential for healing. I have taught Celtic shamanism throughout Europe and the USA and have been continually astonished by the ability of ordinary people to adapt to the teachings and to integrate them into their lives. Often these same people express identical signs of woundedness to those outlined above, and in many cases they have found healing in the practice of shamanism.

In recent years I have begun to amalgamate the two major strands of my work, shamanism and the Arthurian mythos, and have taught a course called 'The Shaman and the Grail' with some success. Many of the techniques and methods of working used on this course will be found in this book, which takes a broadly shamanistic approach to the story of the Grail and the Wounded King, and endeavours to locate the Wounded Healer within each of us. In this way we need not wait for the coming of the Healer – who may come late, or not at all – but find the way to heal ourselves.

Nor is it necessary to be familiar with the techniques of shamanism, or to have practised them before. Everything you need to know will be found in the instructions accompanying each exercise throughout the book, and in the notes which follow the Preface and on pp13–16 of this chapter. With the understanding that comes from working in this way, even the most surface reading of the Grail myth can awaken within us a chorus of voices, clamouring to be heard. We will find that the wounded part of us recognizes the characters and situations in these ancient stories, and that it responds to what it hears. With this we will have taken the first step towards healing ourselves.

I should like to make it clear that I am not advancing a specific healing technique (although ways of accessing the ability to heal oneself will be found throughout the book). Rather I am endeavouring to show how we may enter this particular story, one of a kind recognized as having a healing efficacy, and show some of the ways that working with it can help us to grow and re-connect with our fragmented selves. In effect the healing offered through these pages is a healing of the soul and the spirit, which takes place in the spiritual realm, but which will subsequently manifest in physical terms. Nor is this a book of easy answers. It will not cure everything that may be wrong in your life. What it can do is help you to discover solutions to some of the problems which you may be currently facing. Above all you will be prompted to question your present state of being, to identify and acknowledge various wounds, and to actively seek healing for them through the imagery of the story.

Stories which help us to do this are much needed today. The language of myth and fairy tale is the language of the soul, which is also the language of symbol and dream, and it is to the wounded soul that we must look, again and again, for inward signs of woundedness and for the hope of a cure. As children we understood these stories in a different way; they stepped right into us and took up residence in our innermost hearts. Now we need to re-learn the ways to understand the great myths which are the heritage of our culture and of our inner lives. The stories included here are only a handul of the hundreds which exist, waiting to be read or re-read and understood in a new way. We may have to trick ourselves into accepting the wisdom they contain, telling ourselves we are reading them 'just for pleasure' or 'because we feel nostalgic about them'. Whatever excuse we have to use, the only important thing is to read them with an open heart and an open mind; if we do that they will open themselves to us, and bring healing and nourishment to our thirsty souls. The myths of the Grail are profound; they hold deep truths which offer many kinds of healing, if only we look and feel deeply enough, and let their insights illumine us as we take part in the greatest quest of all.

THE QUEST FOR WHOLENESS

Several writers have looked at the story of the Wounded King in recent years, and have seen it as part of a quest for wholeness, and two in particular deserve to be mentioned here. Both are Jungians, and although I do not necessarily agree with all their findings, I acknowledge the effect their work has had on the development of my own.

The first of these, Roger Woolger, in his illuminating essay 'The Holy Grail: Healing the Sexual Wound in the Western Psyche' (1981), describes the wounded soul and its potential for healing in a memorable passage:

> . . . we must go within, into that unfamiliar land that we can reach in fantasy, dream, and meditation. And our first awareness will be of dead areas and of the ailing, suffering Grail King within. Of head and heart out of harmony with each other. . . A sense of sorrow, of loss, of guilt, of need for penitence. Only if we can go beyond fear and strife . . . within, and are ready to redeem all the lost gentleness and kindness that are the distressed damsels and loathly brides to be married in us all, only then can we find the Grail. (62)

There is much truth in this. We are indeed 'out of harmony', not only with ourselves, but with much of the world. Another symptom of woundedness stems from the realization that we are all essentially alone. The womb from which we emerged is no longer available to us, and the relationships we form with others are perceived as essentially transitory. The wound that results from this is profound and deep; we feel lost and deserted by the universe. Few if any of us who come to this realization ever fully recover from it.

The Grail story, however, teaches us that this realization is false: the Grail itself could not exist if there were not something transcendental to which we could re-connect. The Grail is indeed that which re-connects us to the universal life of the cosmos, and to the earth on which we walk, linking us deeply into the life-force and making us one again with the universe that gave us life. As we begin to work with the characters and situations we find within the Arthurian world, we can indeed learn how to find the 'distressed damsels' of the soul, the lost and fragmented parts of our selves, and to become a healed and fully functioning Grail King.

It is also important to realize that a single individual can embody the aspects of both the Wounded King *and* the Healer, and that therefore we already possess the ability to heal ourselves. To know that we are wounded is half the battle; to know how the wound may be healed is the rest. If you are conscious of both the Wounded King and Perceval within you, you can put one to work on healing the other, thus establishing a relationship of wounded, healer and healed, which deepens your awareness of the wounded nature of creation itself. Thus, as you work towards healing yourself, you are also increasing the degree of healing present within the whole of the cosmos. And if the cumulative effect of our collective wounding becomes overwhelming, as it often seems to do, we would do well to remember that even a small, isolated moment of healing has an ongoing effect which spreads further than we can see.

Recently, Robert A Johnson, in his *The Fisher King and the Handless Maiden* (1993) has considered the wound to be in our ability to 'feel', that is, to express our feelings and to give value to our experience of life. While this is true on one level, there is a much wider degree of woundedness in us, one which permeates a great deal of our lives. Johnson himself seems to understand this, when he says:

> It is very dangerous when a wound is so common in a culture that hardly anyone knows that there is a problem. There is general discontent with our

way of life but almost no one knows specifically where to look for its origin.
(25)

It is my belief that we know very well where to look for the
source of our woundedness: it lies in the fragmentation and suffering of the soul. The Wounded King story reaches to the heart
of this problem, and offers a solution which is potentially accessible to everyone, if only they can be alerted to the nature of the
wound and to its potential cure.

THE WOUNDED LAND

Yet another aspect of the woundedness we all experience
derives from our relationship with the earth. As one of those
who answered the questionnaire noted sagely: 'As humanity is
in a wounded state with the earth, so the earth goes through her
quest for redemption with us'. In the story of the Wounded
King this is expressed by the idea that when the King is
wounded the land over which he rules suffers also. This is in
part an expression of a very old idea, one that we shall examine
in detail later. But it is also an expression of our failure to inter-
act with our environment, over which we have for so long
believed that we possess complete authority, and more generally
in our profound dislocation from the cosmos in which we live.
Older cultures recognized this as a primary source of sickness,
both of the soul and the body. If we become out of phase with
the universe of which we are an integral part, how can we be
either whole or healthy?

All the Grail stories deal with this loss of connectedness,
especially to the healing waters of life. The Waste Land surrounding the Grail King's house is dead because no water flows
there, and the same may be said of our own lives in our
wounded state. But the missing substance is more than simply
water, important though that is; the raw element of life itself is
lacking, in both the land and its ruler, and it is small wonder
that in both the medieval Grail stories and the Celtic traditions
on which they are based, quests to find the Well at the World's
End, or the Fountain of Life, abound.

The tellers of these tales recognized the dislocation which
existed in both people and place. To be cut off from the living
energy of the land was also to be cut off from the magical

power of the Otherworld, and that meant losing the vitality of life itself. This manifests again and again in the tales as images of desolation, soul-hunger and fragmentation. The quest for the Grail and for the healing of land and King is really about the quest for re-connection, for the re-establishment and restoration of what one of the texts calls 'The Courts of Joy'.

When we chose, during the period towards the middle of the 18th century which is sometimes (mistakenly) known as 'the Age of Enlightenment', to place our faith in the sciences, we cut ourselves adrift from the inherited traditions of spirituality which had underpinned our lives for as long as we could remember. This did not happen overnight, of course, but it began a general tendency which has only recently begun to be reversed. In our own time scientific discoveries have begun to reveal that the universe is far more complex than we could ever have imagined, and the resultant effect upon the scientific community has been to demonstrate that borderlands between the almost forgotten realm of the spirit and that of science is far narrower than anyone was prepared to admit. The resulting upsurge of interest in ancient cosmology and spirituality has begun to transform scientific thinking, and has begun to bring us back once again on track with the rest of the universe. Thus in a recent book *Blackfoot Physics: A Journey into the Native American Universe* (1994) its author, the physicist F David Peat, is able to write:

> Modern medical science, with its biochemistry, X-rays, and biopsies, is a marvelous triumph of our technological prowess, yet it is representative of a worldview that has fragmented mind and body, the individual and society, spirit and landscape. (49)

Peat finds the answer to this fragmentation in what he calls indigenous science, that is the natural ways and beliefs of older cultures, here that of the North American continent. Such a position would have been unthinkable as little as ten years ago; but things have moved on a great deal since then, and the scientific community has been forced, not always willingly, to entertain other possibilities.

A science of the Soul is thus once again possible, and with it has come the recognition of the living qualities of the earth. The physical wounding of the environment has begun to be reversed, though whether this has happened in time or not remains to be seen. The important point to realize is that our own wounds are reflected in the wounds we inflict on the earth, and that the healing of the one may (in time) bring about the healing of the other. This alone makes the story of the Wounded King of the utmost importance and relevance to our own time, when we have systematically ravaged the earth for its raw materials with a cavalier disregard for the future. That we will, in time, have to suffer the consequences of that disregard is a fact we need to acknowledge now, just as we need to acknowledge that we ourselves are wounded.

THE BROKEN SOUL

Another way of understanding the relationship of the King and the Land is to recognize this as symptomatic of our inability to connect with our own Soul. We live in an age when many of the organized religions are beginning to fail (in the West at least), and when we have begun to search for something else. This search for a transcendental spirituality motivated the authors of many of the Grail texts composed during the Middle Ages, and it is not at all surprising that these myths should speak to us so forcefully today. For we are also suffering from the same sense of unease, which is a primary sign of soul-loss.

Thomas More has summed this up admirably in his book *Care of the Soul* (1992). Discussing the symptoms which appear with increasing frequency in modern psychological practice, he goes on:

> *All of these symptoms reflect a loss of soul and let us know what the soul craves. We yearn for entertainment, power, intimacy, sexual fulfilment, and material things, and we think we can find these things if we discover the right relationship or job, the right church or therapy. But without soul, whatever we find will be unsatisfying, for what we truly long for is the soul in each of these areas. (44)*

It is my belief that the main reason for the ongoing fascination with the stories of the Grail – and with the practice of shamanism – is because some part of us (or those parts of the soul which long to be reunited with the whole) is aware that it is through stories of this kind, as through the practice of shamanic techniques, that it may be possible to find and retrieve our missing soul-parts. And that with this retrieval will come about a restoration of health and vitality.

Another psychologist, Norman O Brown, says, in his celebrated book *Life Against Death* (1994), 'the aim of psychoanalysis – still unfulfilled and still only half-conscious – is to return our souls to our bodies, to return ourselves to ourselves, and thus to overcome the human state of self-alienation' (19). But it is not that we have lost *all* of our souls, rather that parts of them have become detached from us – through pain, suffering, psychic shock, accident, loss – the same things which, in many instances, are the cause of our wounds.

The concept of soul-fragmentation and soul-loss is perfectly understood among the tribal peoples of the world. Many things are seen as resulting from this, including sickness and several kinds of psychic complaint which we would class as neuroses. Tribal shamans have all kinds of techniques for dealing with this, the most widely used and generally effective being the spirit journey in which the shaman travels out of his body, into the spirit realm, and with the help of spirit-guides and helpers brings back the missing soul-parts and restores them to their clients. This kind of work is seeing a revival today both in Europe and the United States, with practitioners such as Caitlín Matthews and Sandra Ingerman making use of this ancient technique. It is my belief that the damage done to the soul by various aspects of modern living, as well as by circumstances beyond our control, can be similarly treated by working with the imagery and symbolism of the Grail myths, in particular with the story of the Wounded King, who represents so exactly the state of being in which many contemporary Westerners find themselves.

It was for this reason, I now believe, that I was able to help the two people mentioned in the Preface. Both were suffering from soul-loss. That is, both had had parts of their soul driven off by the pain of separation, one through the death of a loved one, the other by the ending of a relationship. Meditating upon the Wounded King helped them because it is a true 'healing' story, containing a powerful account of the cure of both the King himself and of the land over which he rules. This had the effect of calling back those lost soul-parts, which were encouraged to return because of the feeling of warmth and security generated by a direct interaction with the story.

In the course of tracing the inner dimensions of the Wounded King story, and by following the graded exercises which accompany the text, you will be led to relive that experience and, through the acknowledgement of your wounded state and the active seeking of healing, be led to restore your own wounded soul.

This is the healing which is offered by the Grail – restoration and re-connection. You should expect to feel that you are once again in alignment with the rest of the universe; that you are a whole being who can function properly and without losing your way in the miasmas of your wounds; that you can love and be loved unconditionally; and that the emptiness at the centre of your life will once again be filled with warmth and passion and the ability to create.

HOW DOES IT FEEL TO BE HEALED?

This may seem like a strange question to ask here, but not everyone experiences immediate results from this kind of work, and so it is important to realize that one should not give up if an instant response is not forthcoming. More importantly, not everyone *knows* what to feel. This is partly due to the fact that some have been wounded for so long that they cannot imagine feeling any different and are therefore unable to recognize the effects of healing. This is also because most of this work takes place at a soul or spirit level, where the effects are so subtle they are hard to detect at first, and may take time and further inner work to define. A third cause is that most healing happens incrementally, in small changes and inner shifts of direction, which are of their nature difficult to perceive.

So, what does it feel like to be healed? Often, the change is one of atmosphere as much as anything – a lifting of the spirits occurs, along with greater sense of engagement with life, which becomes resultingly less overwhelming and terrifying. Problems which appeared insurmountable suddenly take on a less threatening aspect. This is often accompanied by very real and physical sense of relief. I have heard it described as anything from 'a dark cloud lifting' to 'a sense of release'. The effect is often climactic, mounting to a dizzy sense of euphoria. In the stories which we shall be exploring together this is described as 'the restoration of the Courts of Joy'.

On a purely physiological level the long-term effects of this kind of work are incalculable. As stated above, this is not a therapeutic method as such, though it does help to access your

natural ability to heal yourself, and there is no doubt that
the benefits of this can be considerable. Thus you may find
that certain kinds of illness will simply melt away, while others
begin to respond to treatment which had previously had no
effect. Nothing can be guaranteed, of course, but inner health
can certainly be restored, and there are no harmful side-effects –
only a steady and deeply exciting opening up of the inner life,
and a general widening of our inner visionary capacity.

THE TECHNIQUES IN THIS BOOK

It is important to state here that the methods used here are
somewhat different to those utilized by modern psychoanalyti-
cal practitioners, despite a superficial similarity. The essential
difference is in the belief that the altered states of awareness
experienced by those who adopt these techniques indicate
that the beings they encounter, the places in which they find
themselves, and the events which take place there, are real –
they are not part of the 'subconscious mind' of the individual,
but have a reality of their own, and operate in a world that is
as believable as the one in which we find ourselves, though con-
stituted differently and operating according to its own natural
laws.

This may sound strange to those readers brought up to
believe in the existence of only one reality, which we can see,
hear, smell, touch and taste. But as we continue to explore the
world of the senses, and realize that we know less and less
about what makes us, or the universe around us, 'tick', we open
ourselves up to a wider range of possibilities.

Throughout this book you will find a number of exercises
incorporating ways to work with the imagery and content of
the Grail myth. There are two ways of working: guided visualizations and shamanic journeys. One is comparatively passive,
the other thoroughly active. (See also pp xix–xxi.)

Guided visualization is simply a way of internalizing the
imagery with which we are concerned, and of giving us a direct
experience of what we perceive. It is akin to meditation, except
that you are following a pattern of guided imagery. Shamanic
journey work essentially aims at the same effect, but is more
self-motivated. Instead of passively following a spoken text, we
learn to travel out of our normal sphere of existence, from what

we think of as 'everyday' reality, into what we may call 'subtle' reality; part of your soul undertakes a journey to a kind of 'parallel universe' – the realm of spirit – so that you remain aware of what is happening to you, but are able to access areas of consciousness which are not usually available.

This transition is achieved by entering a light trance-state, usually by listening to a rhythmic sound-source such as a drum, beaten with a particular rhythm and speed. This technique, though simple, is very ancient and extremely effective. I have witnessed some astonishing effects from journey work, and have been privileged to share the experience with many of my students. The same is true of guided visualization work, where one can often watch enthralled as a whole room full of people share a unique experience which is both individually fulfilling and collectively healing.

Neither of these techniques is intrinsically dangerous, provided you are in a reasonably stable frame of mind to begin with. Given the nature of the work, which deals with many kinds of woundedness, a sensible approach is required. Obviously if you are under prescription for drugs or feeling particularly disturbed, you should take due care. These are not techniques to be treated casually, and failure to observe this rule can cause negative effects. In most instances there is no danger to the subject, though the results can be both disturbing and deeply moving; expect to shed tears, either for yourself or others, and do not be dismayed if the changes that occur are other than you may have been led to expect. We are all individuals, and we each respond differently to this kind of work, which operates at a soul level and affects us accordingly. It is important to remember that, as with any quest, undertaken like the Round Table knights and their ladies, a degree of courage is called for. You may find yourself facing your deepest fears, or your worst nightmares, for these are often the outward signs of inner conflict and woundedness.

All the techniques and exercises included have been successfully test-driven by students around the globe. All have proved effective, and though sometimes shattering, can bring both rest and healing to our troubled souls.

I am frequently asked two questions during workshops:

Where do I go when I journey or visualize?
Where do the things I see come from?

The latter is usually accompanied by a statement such as: 'What a great vision. It's a shame I was only imagining it.' The answer to the first question is that when you journey (and to a lesser extent when you visualize) you are moving out of this world and into the realm of subtle reality, which is much the same as this world, only that it is *more* real. In subtle reality, colours, sounds, smells, flavours and textures are vastly enhanced, as is everything we experience. This leads to the second question and its qualifying rider. The imagery comes from a common pool of experience and vision which has been called (among other things) the Otherworld and the Collective Unconscious. These places have their own existence, their own rules and are just as 'real' as anything we see or experience in our daily lives (some might say more so). Thus, when we speak of our imaginations in such slighting terms, we are in fact belittling one of our most powerful tools of self-exploration and healing. To imagine means simply to 'image forth', to give a shape and context to things we would otherwise find inexplicable.

The truth is that our conscious mind acts like a filter, shaping and colouring all that we experience so that it fits into a preconceived pattern of life. Part of the power of journey work and visualization is that it breaks this habit, enabling us to experience an alternative state in which the most subtle changes can (and do) take place. We can be transformed by these experiences in a way that no amount of intellectual consideration can ever do, and in the area of healing work the most profound reaction can take place – particularly at a soul-level – transcending both the usual methods of healing, and the limitations of our physical selves. This is not to say that general medical techniques are of no use to us. Some wounds are best treated by physical skills; you would not go to a shaman to have a broken leg fixed. It is the subtler forms of wounding which respond to a subtler form of healing.

In the workshops on 'The Shaman and the Grail' which I have been offering over the past two years, one of the exercises which I require my students to do consists of making a shamanic journey to the Grail to ask for healing. Usually I divide the group into pairs so that one person journeys for the other in the morning, and the roles are then reversed in the afternoon. This is a well tried method of shamanic work, but I have noticed that when the Grail element is introduced into the equation the results are even more effective than usual. People who have never met before journey for each other and return with information which they could not possibly have known, and which is validated again and again by the person being worked for. It may be no more than that the association of healing with the Grail is itself sufficient to work this miracle, but it seems more likely that there is an inherent power in the Grail which works to heal both the individual and the land at a profoundly deep level.

Exercise 1 The Questing Beast

The first practical step in the journey towards healing is to prepare the way for the work that is to come, and this first exercise is designed to do just that. It is a shamanic exercise which will help you to gain the help of an inner being who will guide and instruct you in the ways of the Otherworld. Generally, in most kinds of shamanic practice, this will take the form of an inner teacher, or more often an animal helper, sometimes called a Power Animal. These are not necessarily actual animals, but spirits who have elected to take this form in order to help us. Once you begin to journey on a regular basis you will find that you quickly establish a sense of these helpers as friends, to whom you can talk in much the same way as to an outer-world friend or colleague. You can learn a great deal from them if you are prepared to listen, and your understanding and awareness will grow deeper with the passage of time.

Generally speaking, the kind of animal helper who comes to us (we do not choose them, they choose us) will be of a common species, for example hawk or hare or bream or tortoise; in this instance, because you are going to be working specifically with the imagery of the Arthurian and Grail myths, you will be seeking out a particular creature, one which actually includes references to a number of animals. This is the Questing Beast, which appears in a number of Arthurian stories, and which exists solely to be sought, or 'quested' after. It is an odd kind of creature, seemingly a composite of several species. It is encountered in the story of Arthur (as told by Thomas Malory) not long after he has become king. Seeking to escape from the attentions of courtiers, the young man goes hunting on his own. Later on, seeking rest and refreshment at a fountain, he hears the approach of what sounds like a pack of hunting dogs:

> And with that the King saw coming towards him the strangest beast that ever he saw or heard of. . . that had in shape a head like a serpent's head, and a body like a leopard, buttocks like a lion, and footed like a hart; and in his body there was such a noise as it had been the noise of thirty couple of hounds questing, and such a noise that beast made wheresomever he went. (Le Morte Darthur, Books 1&9)

Arthur is suitably mystified by this, and it takes the appearance of the wise magical being known as Merlin to explain its purpose to him. The beast exists only to be pursued, and only the right man can achieve the quest. In this we can see an early echo of the search for the Grail. At this point the importance of the Questing Beast is that it can lead us into the Otherworld and that, as our helper, it has access to the places and states of being that we need to visit in our quest for healing. And because it is made up of more than one species of creature, we acquire the help of a potential multitude of beings. For this first, important journey, be prepared to encounter this strange and wonderful being, which may appear in another fashion from the description quoted above, and which will be a composite of more than one species.

Before you begin your journey, have in mind that you are making a visit to the Underworld, the magical realm beneath the earth which is the home of (among others) the Faery races, the Ancestors, and the Lord of the Beasts. These are all described in greater detail in *The Celtic Shaman* and in the handbook to *The Celtic Shaman's Pack* (Element, 1995). For the moment it is sufficient to know that the Ancestors here refer to the Great Dead, the progenitors of our race, rather than any of our own immediate relations (though deceased members of your family may sometimes appear and become your teachers). Most importantly they hold the collective wisdom of our culture, and are the story-tellers who know all the tales worth telling. In Celtic tradition the Lord of the Beasts is represented as a horned man who carries a great club. He sits beneath the Tree of Vision and Tradition, which connects the three worlds of Celtic shamanic tradition: the Firmament or Upperworld, the Circle of Nine or Middleworld, and the In-world or Underworld. When he sees those who have come seeking an animal guide he bangs the bole of the Tree with his club, summoning the helper who is to work with each of us. In this instance, since you are seeking the Questing Beast, you may find it is already awaiting you when you get to the Underworld. If not, and you are greeted by the Lord of the Beasts, ask him to summon the Questing Beast and tell him that you have come for this purpose only. This is merely to prevent confusion, or the appearance of other helpers with whom you are not ready to work. Remember that the Underworld is not a dark and sinister place, but a world within the world we know, lit by stars in the earth, and filled with a multitude of wonders.

To begin your journey proceed as described on pp xix–xxii, then visualize a place in nature where you feel most at home. Next visualize a cave or opening in the ground, or a hole beneath the roots of a tree, and begin your journey from that point, travelling down into the earth and emerging in the Underworld and seeking the help of the Lord of the Beasts. Once you have made contact with the Questing Beast, your task is to get to know it. Perhaps you will simply converse with the Beast on this first meeting, or maybe you will accompany it (perhaps riding on its back) to a place where it has something to show you. Once you feel that you have established the dialogue which will be sustained every time you journey for this particular work, you should take your leave. Be sure to pay attention to anything the Beast says (it may not communicate in words, but in sense impressions, pictures or even scents) and tell it that you are beginning the work of Healing the Wounded King. Be sure to listen for the call-back signal and return gently to ordinary reality. Record anything that happened, and if for any reason you fail to make contact with the Questing Beast on this occasion, try again in a few days and keep trying until you make the breakthrough. In most cases this will be immediate, but if you experience difficulty, keep trying. Alternatively, try journeying aloud. Within a short time you will be journeying with ease and confidence and the wonders of the Otherworld will begin to open up for you.

With this journey you have begun upon the road to healing. The Wounded King has the power to bring healing to your wounds and to transform you. The Grail story as a whole can do this; by looking at one aspect of it we can benefit tremendously, and if nothing else learn more about the nature of our wounded humanity, and perhaps find healing for ourselves in the process. To understand how this may be, it is necessary to look first in detail at the story itself, at some of its variants, and at the mythic structure which underlies it.

2 The Wounded Hero

*It was in the time when the trees bloom, bushes put forth their leaves,
meadows turn green, birds sing sweetly in their language at dawn,
and all things are aflame with joy, that the son of the widow lady
of the lonely wild forest arose . . .*

Perceval Trans by R S Loomis

THE QUEST FOR WHOLENESS

The story of the Grail is the story of a quest for wholeness. It is
also one of the most ancient and powerful tales ever told. No
one can say exactly where or when it first appeared. There are
early, shadowy versions which rise from the massive labyrinth
of Celtic myth, but it assumed the shape with which we are still
most familiar today during the Middle Ages, specifically from
the 12th to the 13th centuries. During this time it became part of
the vast collection of literature known as 'The Matter of Britain',
made up of the Romances of King Arthur and his Knights of the
Round Table, and it has been passed down to us as a wonderful,
magical tale of knightly endeavour, quest and courage, wisdom
and loss, sorrow and triumph; it contains just about every
aspect of our experience as human beings.

Within these stories there are many varied definitions of what
the Grail is, but basically it is a vessel of promise, of healing,
and of transformation. All who come into contact with it are
somehow changed; none doubt for a moment that their quest is
the most wonderful task they will ever undertake. Many will
die on the journey, or get lost amid the perils and distractions
which lie in wait for them around every corner. But at the deepest level of all, the Quest for the Grail is concerned with an even
older search – for healing, and for the gifts of the spirit which
nourish and sustain us all. The Grail offers food for the soul,

and as such we seek it still, determined to overcome every obstacle in our path in order to win this prize that is above all others.

And, just like the knights before us, many of us fail. Many never find their way back to the place where they began, but wander for the rest of their lives, often without realizing it, having forgotten their quest and the reasons for it. This is the experience of life as we know it, and much of it is contained in the stories which you will find within these pages. Read with an open heart and mind, these stories can and do bring healing; they nourish our thirsty spirits and bring us back to an awareness of the road we are travelling.

THE STORY OF THE GRAIL

The earliest text to deal with the Quest for the Grail – and with the Wounded King – is a poem known as *Perceval, ou le Cont del Graal* (*Perceval, or the Story of the Grail*) composed by a 12th-century poet named Chretien de Troyes around 1220 (14). No one knows for sure where the author found this story, or what elements of ancient myth he drew upon in its composition. He had already written five other poems, each with an Arthurian theme, and had thus virtually fathered the great epic cycles of stories which were to follow. The story of the Grail was his last work, and it remained unfinished at the time of his death, adding a further degree of mystery to what was already a mysterious tale. No less than three other authors attempted endings, increasing the overall length of the story by more than three times. Dozens of versions appeared throughout the next two hundred years, each one adding to and changing the story, though always retaining certain essential features. The nature of the Grail itself hardly ever changed, despite appearing in different forms; and the figure of its guardian, the Fisher King, now also referred to as the Wounded King, remained essentially the same. Beyond this, the story underwent a vast variety of changes, becoming indissolubly linked with Christian theology, an element which Chretien's original tale lacked entirely. It became immensely elaborated and was often overlaid with symbolism. But it never strayed far from the original version, which to this day remains its most powerful statement. In re-telling it I have remained faithful to Chretien's original, preferring to leave the variations which were added afterwards until later on in this book, where they will be examined in detail.

Chretien's story of the Grail[1]

A long time ago, when the world was young, a boy grew up alone in the Waste Forest. His mother was a widow, her husband and her two older sons having died in warfare and knightly pursuits. Because of this she had resolved that her youngest child should remain in ignorance of chivalry and knighthood, and so he grew up wild and untamed and knowing nothing of the world outside the forest. He was skilled in the art of hunting, and had learned to throw small javelins with uncanny skill.

One day he went hunting in the forest, and there he chanced to meet a party of knights. When he heard them he thought they must be demons, but once he saw them, all glittering in their armour, he thought they were angels, and fell on his knees by the side of the road as they drew near. The knights spoke to him kindly, asking for news of some other folk who had passed that way recently. But the boy had no thought for anything save their wondrous armour and weapons, and their great horses. He begged them to tell him what they were and whence they came, and thus he learned that they were knights of King Arthur and that they came from the royal court at Caerleon.

At once the boy was filled with longing to go there. He returned home and told his mother of his wishes and she, filled with sorrow, did her best to dissuade him from leaving. When she saw that it was useless to plead with him, she gave him certain advice. If he ever saw a woman in distress he should offer to help her. And, if she was pleased with him, and offered him a kiss, he should accept it – though only if it were offered, for women's favours should never be taken by force. And, if she offered him a ring, then he should accept it forthwith, for this was often a sign of friendship or a pledge of good faith.

With this the boy rode away. As he entered the forest he looked back and saw his mother fall fainting by the gate of their house; but he was so eager to find his way to King Arthur's court that he rode on regardless. Soon after he saw a fine pavilion set up near the road and on entering it found a girl alone within. Half remembering his mother's advice, which he had not really listened to, he helped himself to wine and food and then demanded a kiss from the girl and the ring from her finger – much to her distress. Then he rode on and soon arrived at the royal palace.

As he entered he met a knight in red armour, leaving in some

[1] Passages of particular importance are highlighted.

haste, and carrying in his hand a golden cup. On entering the court he learned that this knight had insulted the king and stolen the cup, spilling wine on the queen as he did so. At once the boy asked to be allowed to pursue the red knight, asking only that he be allowed to keep his armour and weapons if he could get them. Sir Kay, the king's seneschal, mocked him, but a girl who had not laughed for years, did so now and prophesied that the youth would one day be famous. Kay struck her for her insolence and was reprimanded by the king.

The boy went forth and overtook the red knight, whom he killed by throwing a javelin into his eye. Then, with difficulty, he removed the fallen man's armour and mounted his charger. Riding on he arrived at a great castle and was well received by its master, an experienced knight named Gorneman de Gorhaut. Upon hearing the boy's story the old knight offered to teach him the ways of chivalry and knighthood. He found him a willing pupil and in a while made him a knight.

The boy was now eager to depart, but before he left Gorneman gave him some advice: always to help those who needed it, and not to talk too much, or ask too many questions, lest people thought him foolish or mad. The boy gave him thanks and rode on his way.

Soon he arrived at the castle of Beaurepair, which belonged to a beautiful maiden named Blanchflor. The boy fell in love with her and she with him, and on learning that she was being persecuted by a knight named Engygeron, who sought her hand and her property for his master, he determined to take up her cause. He soon defeated the knight, and afterwards his master, and restored to Blanchflor her lands and freedom.

His thoughts now turned to his home and to the sight of his mother falling by the entrance to the house, and he resolved to go there to see that she was well and to tell her of his adventures. Though reluctant to let him go, Blanchflor saw that she could not restrain him, and the boy set out at once. He soon found that he had lost his way, and after wandering in the forest for a while he came to a fierce, deep stretch of water, which he was afraid to cross. Just then he became aware of a little boat floating downstream, in which were two men. As he watched they anchored in the midst of the stream and one of them commenced fishing. The boy called out to them, asking where he might cross the water. The fisherman told him that there was no fording place near at hand, but that he was welcome to find lodging at his house that night. He gave instructions to the boy to go upstream, though a cleft in a rock, from the summit of which he would see a house in a valley below him.

The boy did as he was told, but at first could see nothing. Then he spied a tower rising above the trees and made for it. He found himself at a beautiful house where he was made welcome and ushered into a great hall where he saw an elderly man sitting upright in a large bed. The man bade him welcome, apologizing for not getting up and inviting the boy to sit beside him on the bed.

While they were talking a youth entered with a beautiful, jewel-hilted sword which he offered to the lord of the house. It had been sent by his niece, with the understanding that he bestow it wherever he liked, so long as it was put to good use. It was one of three swords made by a famous smith.

The old lord declared that the sword was destined for his guest, and fastened it on him personally. Then they fell to conversing again. *While they were talking a boy came into the court carrying a white lance. A drop of blood issued from its tip and ran down as far as the place where the youth held it. The youth was astonished at the sight, but remembering the advice of Gorneman he forbore to ask its meaning. At this moment two more youths entered, carrying two golden candlesticks in each of which burned ten candles. A girl came in with them, carrying a grail between her hands. Such a great light came with her that the candles lost their brightness as though they were stars dimmed by the rising sun. Next came another girl bearing a silver trencher in her hands. The grail was golden and covered with the most splendid jewels. As with the bleeding spear, these objects were carried through the hall, past the bed where the old lord sat, and into another chamber. All this the boy saw and dared ask nothing of its meaning.*

Food was now brought to them, and after they had dined the old lord was carried to his chamber. The boy remained in the hall and slept on the great bed. He was greatly puzzled by the things he had seen, and resolved to ask one of the servants in the morning. But, when he awoke, he could find no one. The whole castle seemed deserted, and his arms were laid out ready for him. When he left the hall he found the gates open and his horse already saddled and waiting. As he rode forth the drawbridge rose behind him, and though he called out no one answered.

Bewildered, the boy rode on until he found fresh tracks in the earth. These he believed to belong to the people from the castle, and so he followed them, expecting at every moment to see familiar faces. But instead he found a maiden weeping beside the body of her dead lover. The boy asked who had done this terrible deed, but the girl was distracted and could only comment on the fact that his horse seemed fresh, though he must have come far since there was no shelter to be had near at hand. When the boy said that he had come from a fine house close by the maiden at once declared that he must have spent the night in the house of the Fisher King.

The boy told her that he had indeed spent the night in the house of a man whom he had first seen fishing, though he did not know if he was a king or not. The girl assured him that the man was indeed a king, and that he spent his time fishing because he had been wounded in battle by a javelin through both thighs and could engage in no other sport since he could no longer ride on a horse. The girl then asked if he had seen the spear, and the other wonders, and if he had asked about them. The boy admitted that he had indeed seen them, but that he had failed to ask any such questions. At once the girl berated him for his failure to speak out, for if he had done so the Fisher King would have been healed, and could rule over his lands again. Much good would have come to the boy also, but from his failure would come much sorrow and pain, not only to himself but to others also. She then asked him his name, and the boy, who did not know it, guessed that he was called Perceval.

Then the girl announced that she was his cousin, who had lived at their house in the forest when he was an infant, though he had since forgotten her. And she told him that his mother was indeed dead, being unable to bear the grief at his departure to what she believed would be certain death.

Filled with sorrow and shame, Perceval declared his intention of seeking out the knight who had killed the girl's lover. In answer she warned him that the sword given him by the Fisher King would break when he most needed it. Perceval set forth at once and soon after came upon a woman in the rags of a once fine dress riding on a spavined mare. Perceval discovered that she was the same girl from whom he had taken the ring and whom he had kissed on his way to Arthur's court. Her jealous lover had punished her for what he saw as a betrayal by making her ride always before him in the same old clothes. The knight himself arrived at this point, and was revealed as the one whom Perceval was already pursuing. The two knights fought, and Perceval quickly defeated the jealous knight, despite the fact that the beautiful sword given him by the Fisher King broke in the process. Perceval then made the jealous knight promise to repay the suffering he had caused his lady, and to report to King Arthur for judgement.

When they heard of Perceval's deeds, the king and most of the court set out in search of him. Perceval himself had also set out again, in search of more adventures. On the way he saw a wild goose attacked by a hawk. Some of its blood dropped on the snow which had fallen that morning, and the boy was entranced by the sight, which reminded him of the red and white of Blanchflor's complexion.

While he stood thus the first of Arthur's knights came in sight and tried to speak to him. Perceval was so distracted that he at first ignored them, and when Sir Kay tried to arouse him Perceval absently knocked him from his horse, breaking his arm and thus, incidentally, avenging the blow to the maiden who had laughed to see him and who had prophesied his future fame. Finally roused from his daydream, the young knight greeted King Arthur and was escorted back to the court in triumph.

This was to be short-lived however, for next day there arrived a woman on a mule who was the ugliest creature that had ever been seen at the court. Her hair was black and snake-like, her skin dark as a Saracen's, her eyes were as small as a rat's, her teeth yellow, her nose was like a cat and she had a beard like a goat. Her back was humped and twisted and her legs as curved as withy wands. She rode up boldly and greeted everyone there except Perceval. Him she cursed and took to task for his failure to ask the

all-important questions concerning the bleeding lance and the grail. 'For,'
she said, 'wretched is he who sees an opportunity and looks for a better
one.' And she went on to tell him that if he had asked about the lance and
the worthy man who was served by the grail then all the ills of the Fisher
King and his lands would have been set right. But because he had failed to
do so, 'Ladies will lose their husbands, lands will be laid waste, girls will
be left in distress and orphaned, and many knights will die; all these evils
will happen because of you.'

The hideous lady then proceeded to announce a whole series of
adventures, which various of the knights elected to attempt, while
Perceval, greatly cast down by her words, swore that he would not
rest in any one place for more than a night until he had found his
way back to the house of the Fisher King and asked concerning the
wonders that he had seen there.

The story now turns away from Perceval for most of the
remainder of the poem, dealing with the adventures of Gawain.
Only one other episode need concern us here. In this we learn
that Perceval spends the next five years wandering in the
wilderness, sending many errant knights to King Arthur, but
never finding his way to the house of the Fisher King, until in
time he forgets both who he was and the nature his task. Then:

It was on Good Friday that Perceval was riding along, when he
beheld a group of knights and ladies going in procession along the
way. The women were bare-foot and the knights rode with their
hoods covering their faces and bore neither armour nor weapons.
When they saw Perceval riding along fully armed they asked in
wonder if he knew what day it was. When he answered that he did
not, they reminded him of the mysteries of Easter, and bade him lay
aside his weapons. Contrite that he had lost his way for so long,
and that he had forgotten his purpose, Perceval asked where they
had come from and was told they had been visiting a certain holy
hermit who lived close by. Perceval set out at once for the chapel
where the hermit lived and when he entered there fell on his knees
and wept for a long time. Hearing him, the hermit came forth, and
Perceval poured out the whole story. When he was done the hermit
sighed heavily and told him that he was in fact his uncle, his
mother's brother, as was the Fisher King also, so that all were
related. And he told the young knight that his mother's death was
upon his conscience and had prevented him from asking the all-
important questions which would have healed the king and his
lands.

Then Perceval was truly filled with sorrow, and wept for a long
time. But the hermit forgave him and gave him penance and told
him to be of good cheer. And on that Good Friday he heard mass
and received the sacraments and was rested.

After this we hear no more of Perceval. The text turns again to the adventures of Gawain, which we shall examine later. Chretien's poem ends, literally half-way through a sentence, and is taken up by various continuators, only one of whom actually brings the story to something like a satisfactory conclusion. In this, the third of the continuations, each of which is as long or longer than the original, we learn more of the procession and of the wounded Fisher King. The Bleeding Spear, we are told, is that which the centurion Longinus used to pierce the side of Christ on the cross. The Grail is the holy vessel used to celebrate the Last Supper, and which subsequently, in the hands of a disciple named Joseph of Arimathea, caught some of the blood which flowed from the side of Christ when his body was taken down from the cross and prepared for burial in the same Joseph's tomb. Both are thus sacred objects, stained with the blood of Christ, holy relics which stem from the fountainhead of Christianity.

This is the essential story of the Grail and the Wounded King. I have given it here in some detail partly because we shall refer back to this version throughout, and also because there have been many retellings which have frequently altered the structure and even some of the most important details, which have been bent to fit various theories. In fact the story needs no rewriting to make its points obvious, and as we shall see it contains virtually all we need to know of the central story, though we shall look to other texts to flesh out certain areas and details.

WHOM DOES THE GRAIL SERVE?

One person who responded to the questionnaire wrote that: 'I could see how the Grail procession was meant to stir a seed deep within the heart of Perceval and within the heart of the hearer of the tale. A memory of connection warming the seed of a rich and fertile land. And how within my own life that seed had been stirred and warmed, and since that moment I've searched and asked, what does this mean? I realized that [the need] to honour that stirring, to answer its calling, is imbedded within my heart and mind and [that] it has given me life. For Perceval to have turned away from that procession or me to have turned away from that inner procession, a wound would have been driven deeper and a land laid waste once more.'

We have always needed stories that can bring forth a response like this, myths which tell us the old half-forgotten secrets which were once such an important part of our lives. Living towards the end of the 20th century we have become, to a large extent, symbolically illiterate, unable to see behind the stories which tell of an unending search and a terrible hunger: the search for healing and the hunger for wholeness, for a return to the original state in which we somehow know we rightly belong. It is this primal sense of disconnectedness that is the cause of so much of our woundedness. We know there is something missing in our lives, but all too often we do not know what, or how we can rediscover it. And so we are filled with suffering which we bear as best we can, or we spend our time grumbling, and make do with the nearest thing we can to happiness. How many times have we heard others express this same feeling, and thought: 'Yes, that's true. I feel the same', and yet were unable to speak out or ask the questions which might set us free? This is why, in the Grail story, one of the most important actions of the hero is to ask a question: 'Whom does the Grail serve?'

In most of the accounts of the story the answer is 'the Wounded King', but the underlying truth is that the Grail serves everyone; or, to put it another way, it serves *you*. Many of us, like the king himself, cannot ask the question for ourselves, but must wait for the Healer to ask it for us. Often we do not even know what the question is, or of whom we should ask it. And even if we manage to overcome these obstacles, we are then faced with the problem of service itself. Some people cannot find healing because they do not like to be served by others, or because they perceive service as something to which they are entitled, and try to wrest it from others without respect or forethought. Ultimately, the mystery is one of exchange: the Grail serves us as we serve the Grail. This is an important part of the healing, just as it is the asking of the question which triggers the reflex that will ultimately bring healing to the wounded soul and the wounded earth.

There is a paradoxical sequence underpinning all of this: the Grail is here from the beginning, though it comes and goes; it is ever-present, but must be sought for; it is available to all, but is kept hidden in a mysterious place; it serves all, yet only those who know the right question can unlock its healing power; it heals us but we must be wounded in order to find that healing. These are the mysteries which lie at the heart of the Grail.

The Hero's Task

If we break down the story of Perceval, we find that it falls naturally into a number of episodes which reflect the experience of the hero at a very deep level, and which is mirrored in the lives of all who seek the healing of the Grail. The pattern may be expressed as follows:

- The hero rebels against the constraints of an ordinary life
- Sets forth in quest of something wondrous he has heard of
- Recognizes the wound, but cannot speak of it
- Is spurred on to act by the Hideous Damsel
- Endures hardship and separation
- Returns to the castle and asks the Question
- Brings healing and is himself healed.

At the beginning of the story Perceval is completely at home in the forest. He has no idea that there is anything missing from his life. He knows nothing of the society of men, of fatherly love and affection, or of the companionship of brothers. Then he meets Arthur's knights, and this seemingly accidental encounter opens him to a realm of possibilities which he is eager to experience for himself. He hastens back to his mother and announces his intention of departing. She, knowing there is nothing she can do to prevent this, and that her desire to protect her son from the outside world has failed, gives him the best advice she can; though this is based on a limited view of life, which has been shaped by her personal suffering.

When Perceval escapes to the forest every day he is already trying to assert his independence; with the appearance of the knights he is given the means to break free. He seems heartless, caring nothing for his mother's feelings, yet he is truly fighting for the possession of his own soul, part of which has been appropriated by his mother, and which he will indeed leave behind when he sets out on his momentous journey.

He is taking the first step towards the recognition of his own wounded state. He knows, without thinking, that he can be himself, and he is filled with excitement at the prospect. This causes him to behave in an impetuous manner, as his encounter with the Maiden of the Tent shows. This is his first contact with the feminine outside his home, and he has no idea how to behave. Unfortunately, he misunderstands his mother's advice, which he had not really heard in his excitement, and instead of dealing gently with the girl he forcefully demands a kiss and takes her ring without permission; acts which are to cause trouble for the Maiden herself, and ultimately for Perceval. His wound has cut him off from the outer world, crippling the natural instinct which would normally govern his behaviour, and leaving him without the sense of self which is such a vital part of human expression.

Hastening on, he arrives at Arthur's court and is at once recognized by the girl who has not spoken for years. She prophesies his future fame and receives a blow from the arrogant seneschal Kay. It is significant that Perceval receives his first recognition outside his home environment from a woman. Most of his actions to date have been in an effort to assert his masculinity, and to carve out a place for himself in the world of knights and chivalry. But at virtually every point on his journey he encounters women who give him direction, though typically he fails to notice this until it is almost too late.

This is a situation which occurs throughout much of the Arthurian cycle. Again and again we see the devotion of the knights to womankind, at variance with their customary aggressiveness towards the world at large. In every way, from Lancelot's unswerving devotion to Guinevere to the simplest act of kindness or protectiveness carried out by the Round Table knights during their adventures, the power of women is silently acknowledged, even while it is also systematically derided and feared in the shape of such negative-seeming characters as Morgan le Fay or Nimue, who are represented as Arthur's greatest adversary and Merlin's nemesis respectively. Yet, as has often been noted before, salvation, for a man, almost always comes by way of a feminine carrier, of which perhaps the most famous example is Beatrice in Dante's *Divine Comedy*, where the presence of the poet's love acts as both guide and inspiration throughout his long journey through the levels of Hell, Purgatory and Heaven. And thus in the Grail story it is a woman (the Grail Princess) who bears the mystical vessel, and a woman (the Hideous Damsel) who challenges the wandering knights to take up their quest again. Both are images of what, in

Jungian terms, is called the *anima*, the feminine consciousness that exists within all men, just as the *animus*, or masculine consciousness, exists within all women. Perceval is offered help by these inner beings at almost every step of the way. Typically, as with most men, he fails to notice.

Having reached the court and been acknowledged by the silent girl, Perceval now undertakes his first real adventure. Not surprisingly, perhaps, in the light of his attachment to the feminine, it is on behalf of the Queen, Guinevere, that he sets out to exact reparation for the blow which the Red Knight has dealt, and to bring back the golden cup he has stolen. This in a way predicts the later quest for the Grail, and is an echo of the theft of the cups from the Damsels of the Wells, of which we shall hear more in Chapter 4.

His first adventure is successful, more by accident than design and, having tasted the heady excitement of battle and conquest, Perceval is eager to set out again. He then meets the older knight, Gorneman, who acts as a surrogate father, teaching him the ways of chivalry and knighthood: how to put on armour, fight with sword and lance, and how to ride a horse properly. It is at this point that Perceval receives his real initiation into manhood, and it is from Gorneman that he also acquires his next piece of advice: to help those in need, but not to ask too many questions. This advice, given with sincerity, is to be his undoing. It re-enforces his inability to act, which derives from his years in the protective womb of the forest; and it will prevent him from carrying out his greatest task, the healing of the Wounded King, which is so closely linked to Perceval's own quest for wholeness.

His next encounter with the feminine is with Blanchflor. He experiences the pain of love for the first time, and has his own feelings reciprocated. Interestingly, it is here that we find a kind of pre-image of the Waste Land. Blanchflor has been besieged for some time by the knight Engygeron, and her lands have suffered accordingly and been laid waste.

Everywhere [Perceval] . . . went he found the streets waste and the houses in ruins, with not a man or woman anywhere. There were two churches in the town which had both been abbeys: one of nuns, lost and fearful, the other of monks, confused, bewildered. He found these churches well adorned neither with ornament nor tapestry; instead he saw their walls crumbling and broken, their towers open to the sky; and the doors of houses hung open at night as they did by day. No millstone ground, no

oven baked in any part of the town, and there was neither wine nor morsel
of bread. . . Thus he found the castle waste. . . (14)

Presented with these images of desolation, and assaulted by his
new-found feelings of love, Perceval desires only to help the
lady of the castle. He puts his newly honed skills to work and
defeats those who would have taken Blanchflor by force. For a
moment he is on course, following the path that was intended
for him, combining both his masculine and feminine energies in
the service of good. But almost immediately he is knocked off
balance by the memory of his mother, whom he had last seen
fainting at the entrance to their house, but whom he has
scarcely thought of since. Unable to commit to his love for
Blanchflor he turns aside and sets out in search of home.

At once he realizes he is lost. He has taken his foot off the
path and the forest has reclaimed him. Yet it is at this point that
the Wounded Hero encounters the Wounded King. As so often
happens in our own lives, just as we are feeling most deeply
bereft and alone, something occurs which renews our self-belief
and sets us on the right road again. Often this takes the form of
a casual encounter which may change us forever. In Perceval's
case it is not to be so simple. He has first to undergo a supreme
test of self-awareness, an opportunity to act in which he will fail
dismally, precisely because he has no understanding of his life
purpose. At this point he is still incomplete; like so many of us
he has lost the innate sense of direction which enables us to
steer a course through the shoals of a seemingly endless sea.

Fittingly for someone in this condition he sees a man fishing
from a small boat in the midst of a wide and tumultuous river.
The water rushes by on all sides, but the fisherman and his boat
are still and calm in the centre. Perceval calls out to the fisherman, asking for a way across. He is told there is no fording
place nearby, but that he is welcome to stay in the fisherman's
house that night. Faced with what seems to be an unsurmount-
able barrier, Perceval is willing to accept the invitation to rest in
a place that offers stability. Like many of us who reach this
point in our journey, Perceval needs a soul-friend, someone
with whom he can find rest and refreshment, and perhaps
words of homely wisdom.

And so he comes to the house of the Grail, and witnesses
the strange and wonderful procession of objects; the lance,
from which run drops of blood, and the mysterious vessels, from

which issues a light so powerful that the candles carried in the procession seem like stars whose radiance is dimmed by the rising sun. Perceval wonders greatly at this, but he remembers Gorneman's advice and fails to ask the meaning of what he sees. This is because, as we too may frequently have done, he fails to recognize the solution to his own problem. Had he asked he would not only have released the Wounded King, but also found the answer he was seeking: the healing of his own inner wounds. As it is, he wakes in the morning to find the castle strangely deserted, his horse saddled and his armour and weapons laid out ready. As he departs, expecting at every moment to meet someone from the castle, the drawbridge slams shut behind him. Though he still does not know it, he has lost an opportunity for healing which will not come again for some time. We too can stumble upon ways to heal ourselves but, failing to recognize these for what they are, find ourselves pushing onward, getting ever further from the source of true healing.

Wandering onwards, Perceval enters a period when he will begin to earn some of the qualities that have been hitherto missing from his life. First he encounters a weeping girl, who is astonished that he looks so fresh when there is nowhere close by where he could have found shelter. When he tells her of the castle, however, she acknowledges its existence at once, and begins to question him. This seeming inconsistency is not without significance. The Grail Castle is always close by, but it is not always visible to those who seek it. Indeed it often seems that the seeker must take the longest possible road to reach somewhere that was next door all the time.

Perceval learns more about his host of the previous night, how he had been wounded through both thighs and could only find rest in fishing. If Perceval had asked about the procession not only would the Fisher King have been healed but good would have come to himself also. The girl turns out to be his own cousin, who had lived in his house when he was an infant. She tells him that his mother has died of the grief caused by his departure, and asks him his name. Perceval, who has hitherto been referred to in the text only as 'the boy', confesses that he is uncertain of his own name, but 'guesses' that it is Perceval.

This is a pivotal point in the story. Perceval has taken the first real step towards discovering who he is and to acknowledging his wounds. With this will come, in time, the healing he needs to make him whole. As he confesses his ignorance he is gifted with an inner twinge of knowledge – his name. If, as some authorities have suggested, it means 'pierce the vale' this is entirely appropriate. In this moment of recognition his own road towards healing has begun, though he has no real awareness of this as yet.

From here the story begins to unravel itself. Perceval opts to avenge himself on the knight who had murdered his cousin's lover. When he catches up with the felon he discovers him to be the protector of the Maiden of the Tent, and learns about the effect of his earlier unthinking actions. The knight, discovering that his lady had received a visitor who had helped himself to her ring and demanded a kiss, had forced her to ride before him on a broken-down horse, wearing the same dress until it was almost falling from her. Thus Perceval is given the opportunity to put right his earlier mistake. He defeats the knight, and makes him promise to make full reparation to his lady, and to request judgement in the matter of the dead knight from Arthur. Thus we see the effects of Perceval's ill-advised actions, which change the Maiden of the Tent's life for the worse. Indeed this whole section of the story deals with the results of impetuous and unthinking actions which hold up the progress towards healing; Perceval is at last beginning to solve the riddle of life which will lead to his own healing, as well as that of the Wounded King.

Perceval wanders on in search of his old home, until he sees where a wild goose has been killed by a hawk. Drops of blood in the snow remind him of Blanchflor and he becomes so abstracted that when Arthur and some of his knights arrive, looking for him, he absently unhorses Kay, and thus avenges the blow given to the girl who had not spoken for years until she saw him. Here we seem to be seeing the working out of destiny, and the balancing of positive and negative effects. Though Perceval is still capable of being sidetracked, he has begun to express himself instinctively.

It seems that Perceval's star is in the ascendant. He has defeated all who oppose him, he has won the love of a beautiful woman, he is honoured at Arthur's court. But in fact this is only the beginning of his most severe trials. As so often in our own lives, when the moment of greatest success seems hollow, the effects of woundedness reach out to pull us back to earth. Haunted by the memory of the Wounded King, and by the death of his mother, he feels empty. It is at this moment, when he might have settled for the life of a knight and forgotten everything else, that a new figure enters his life. This is the Hideous Damsel, who arrives at the court and berates him for his failure to ask the all-important question concerning the Grail and the Lance. Because of him women will be widowed, lands laid waste, girls raped and men killed. It is a terrible load to lay upon anyone, and Perceval is indeed brought low by it.

And yet, despite this, he is also being offered another chance to find healing. Sometimes we require a shock of this kind, delivered with merciless grace, to shake us free of our habitual lives. It is all too easy to settle back into a state of normality, accepting what fate, or circumstance, has meted out to us. The first step towards healing is to recognize this, and in some dim, half-hidden chamber of his soul Perceval does just this. He instinctively breaks free of the dream state – represented by the blood in the snow episode – and prepares to set out again, to undergo whatever tests and trials may lie in wait for him, urged on by the Hideous Damsel, the dark and powerful aspect of the feminine which he has been seeking to deny ever since he left the forest.

But even now his way is dogged by doubt and uncertainty, by wrong turnings and forgotten promises. For a time he goes about behaving exactly as a knight was expected to, apparently following his destiny, doing a good job. But it is all hollow; he knows there should be more, but is afraid to search his own wound too deeply. In this he is like many of us. We become aware that we are wounded, but are afraid to take the necessary action to seek healing. Facing this fear is another of the most important steps towards healing the wound, and very often we are unable to do so without help; we need a Healer ourselves. And this is just what happens in the story. Perceval wanders for years, lost and gradually forgetting his true task. Then he meets a party of pilgrims on their way to celebrate Easter at the chapel of a famous hermit. It is they who remind him of his true task, and are instrumental in setting his feet once again on the right path. Nor does it matter that they are celebrating a Christian feast – thought it happens to be one in which the symbolism of the Grail looms large – it is sufficient that they bring Perceval to the hermit, who of course turns out to be the Wounded King's brother and Perceval's own uncle. It is now that some of the final pieces fall into place. Perceval discovers that the Fisher King is related to him, and is told that it was guilt over the death of his mother (self-blame is another of the prime signs of woundedness) which had prevented him from finding his way back to the Grail Castle.

The hermit then grants Perceval forgiveness, which we all need if we are to progress in our quest for healing. Often this means forgiving ourselves, acknowledging that we are not perfect, that we have behaved wrongly towards others, that we have occasionally failed in our most serious undertakings. If not done, like the asking of the question, this can be an immense stumbling block to discovering the way back to a whole state. Perceval, thus set free of his greatest burdens, can proceed with the task in hand, the healing of the Wounded King and the Waste Land. Even though Chretien's story breaks off before the end, it is not difficult to foresee the outcome: Perceval will transcend his own state of woundedness, and will make a new beginning. When he has healed the King and the land, set free the waters, both within himself and the king, he will be able to function properly. He will marry Blanchflor and father a family. He will become a whole individual for the first time.

The everyday parallels to this are obvious. Acknowledging your wounds, and recognizing them for what they are, is a hugely important step in the healing process. Once we have succeeded in doing this, many of the obstructions to our work will melt away, leaving us free to begin the process that will take us into a state of wholeness. The following exercise, a guided visualization, is intended to help you to do this, and to experience something of the same inner dynamic by which Perceval reached this point in his journey.

Exercise 2 The Hero's Journey

Prepare yourself for meditation in the usual way. When you are relaxed and centred allow your surroundings to fade. You are Perceval. You have left behind the forest world and your childhood home; you have journeyed to Arthur's court and successfully achieved the adventure of the Red Knight. King Arthur has rewarded you well, and you are a Knight of the Round Table. Now you prepare to set forth on a new journey. You put on your gleaming armour and mount your fine horse. Then you ride forth from Camelot the Golden in search of fresh adventure. The air is warm and full of the scents of summer.

The road lies before you like a ribbon of light stretching out across the land. Trees and hedgerows line the way, and the sound of bird song echoes in your ears. It is a perfect day; you feel strong and full of energy and the burning desire to prove that you are the best knight of Arthur's splendid fellowship. And yet, as you ride along, feeling the warm strength of your mount beneath you, the familiar weight of your sword in its sheath at your hip, you become aware that there is something wrong. There is a sense of emptiness within you. You know that your purpose is to put right any wrongs you encounter, to help those who need it – but suddenly you cannot think of a reason why you should do these things. Who is going to notice if you simply ride away, find a quiet place to stay, and live out the rest of your days in comfort? With this comes another awareness. Your mind goes back to the old carefree days in the forest, when you roamed at will, hunting for food for yourself and your mother, swimming in the cool stream which flowed beneath the trees. You were happy and carefree then, without responsibilities or worries. At the end of the day you could return home and there was always a hot meal and fresh clothes and a warm bed in which to sleep. Now you have exchanged all these for a life of danger and hardship, where you must often sleep out on the rough ground and where you never know where your next meal will come from.

The bright day is suddenly overcast. Fear grips you, and you begin to think of all the terrible things that could happen to you, the dangers that may lurk around the next bend in the road. In vain you remind yourself that you are Perceval, a Knight of the Round Table; that you successfully slew the Red Knight and took back the golden cup to the Queen. Arthur's voice, praising you, seems to speak from another time and place, far away from this terrible land in which you find yourself. In vain you try to form a prayer, but there is no comfort to be had from this. You feel like a small child, abandoned by its parents, frightened and alone in a vast and hostile universe . . . In terror you fling yourself from the back of your horse and run to hide behind a great tree. You are shaking from head to foot and sweat runs off you.

For a time you crouch in the protective shadow of the tree. Then you hear the sound of hoofs approaching along the way. At first this only causes your fear to grow stronger, but at length you are able to bring yourself to look around the tree to see who, or what, is coming closer. You see a young woman on a white horse approaching, and at once your fear dissipates somewhat. You emerge from behind the tree and see that your horse is grazing nearby. The young woman rides closer and reins in her mount. She looks down at you and smiles and your fears vanish in the warmth of her gaze. She asks you your name, and when she hears that you are Perceval she tells you that she has come to find you and asks you to follow her. You mount your horse and ride at her side along the road, and as you do so your spirits lift. Life seems good again and the terrors of the morning seem far away.

You ride on with the young woman until you reach a fine manor house which lies snugly among a brake of sheltering trees. It reminds you somewhat of your own home and you feel comfortable there as you are made welcome, your horse led away to the stables, you are helped to unarm and given water to wash yourself and wine and food to eat. And all the while your young companion speaks gently of this and that, and seems to be watching you, as if waiting for you to say or do something – you know not what.

At length when supper is ended your hostess bids you follow her into a side chamber. There you see a huge mirror upon one wall, from which the images of yourself and the young woman look back.

'I have brought you to this place so that you may see what you need to see,' your hostess tells you. 'I saw your pain upon the way, and knew that you were Perceval and that you had need of healing. Look now within the mirror and see the truth.'

As she speaks you become aware that your own image in the mirror is changing. Suddenly you see that there are wounds all over you, as though you had just fought in a long and bloody battle. You feel no pain, but a great sorrow clouds your mind. This is worse than the terrors of the road, and yet as you look you see that the wounds are only superficial, and there comes into your mind the idea that you might be healed quite quickly if you were to place yourself in the hands of a skilled physician.

You turn to the young woman. 'I am wounded. How can I be healed?'

She smiles her warmest smile. 'Even now,' she says, 'By asking this question, you have begun your own healing. The rest will follow. Then you may begin your true work, which is the healing of others. This is the true way of the hero, not simply the acts of bravery of which you are capable, but the acts of healing also.'

Her words give you far greater comfort than you would have believed possible only a short while ago. As you look in the mirror you see your wounds begin to heal – though you know that they go deeper than they seem to, and that there are still many ways to go, many trials to undertake, before you can call yourself fully healed. Gradually the scene begins to fade, and you become aware that you are back on the road, lying beneath the tree where you had taken shelter in your fear. Your horse crops the grass peacefully nearby and the sun still shines from a clear sky. You get up and re-mount and set forth again on the road. Your heart is high again, but you are tempered by the knowledge that, like all who follow the path of the hero, you are wounded, though not always in ways that can be seen. You wonder who the young woman was, or if it was all a dream, and still thinking of this the scene slowly fades from your inner sight and you awaken to find yourself back where you began your journey. Take a moment to restore yourself fully to everyday consciousness and write down any thoughts or realizations that may have come about as a result of your journey.

HEALING THE HERO

When we look at Chretien's story we can immediately see that it relates to our own lives in all kinds of ways. Perceval comes from the Waste Forest in this version. This means that he has experienced the dry and desolate place, which is just as much an inner state as an outer one. He is wounded by the deaths of father, brothers, and soon, mother – for which he is in some sense to blame. Through this, and through the experiences he undergoes, he becomes a wounded healer, the promised one who will one day restore the Fisher King and his wounded land. But he must suffer more yet, for he has mistaken the advice of both his mother and of Gorneman, so that he cannot do what is required of him. He is behaving very like so many of us today – frozen and bewildered, we cannot create the circumstances we need to bring about either our own healing or that of those we encounter on our way, and who need it as much (or more) than ourselves.

Perceval must undergo further hardships and trials until he is deepened by his experience of the Wound, growing wise through suffering, until at last he is reminded of who he is and what his role is in the work of the Grail. Until then the best he can do is guess at his name (and nature); he wanders blindly from place to place, a victim of whatever fate throws his way. Every time he tries to act – as when he departs for Arthur's court in a hot-headed fashion, or when he decides to leave his lovely Blanchflor and search for fresh adventures – he is utterly unprepared for what happens. In other words he resembles many of us, who set out on our own journey through life unaware of what lies ahead. Like Perceval, we may sometimes wander for many years before we discover our true purpose. We have to experience the nature of the Wound before we can become healers ourselves.

We can see that part of Perceval's quest is to reconcile his masculine and feminine halves, and to acknowledge the barriers which their dislocation throw up in his life. He struggles to leave the safe harbour of his home and the protection of his mother; he meets women whom he either treats casually, or with whom he falls in love; he is spurred on to the completion of his task by his cousin and by the Hideous Damsel. On the other side he is aided by King Arthur, by Gorneman, and by his uncle the Hermit, each of whom, in his own way, advances his masculine self, as well as nurturing his growing self-esteem.

Perceval's teachers thus each take a share of his integration: this may be expressed as follows:

- his mother
- his uncle
- experience

can be said to foster:

- his feminine self
- his masculinity
- the integration of the two

He must work through the instruction which each one of them has to offer before he can reach a point of completion that will enable him to move on. But this is no easy task, for throughout the story Perceval retains his simplicity: the complex response is missing from his character. This is both a problem and an advantage: his simplicity and determination to cling to his mother's advice prevent him from asking the Question. He blindly accepts all that occurs; he is adrift and directionless (he let his horse wander at will); the benefit is that when he has integrated the two sides of his nature he is at last able to ask the question.

But does he do so with understanding, or is this simply another response, programmed into him by his inexperience of the world? It is so easy to believe one is doing the right thing because it is also the accepted thing. Everything Perceval has experienced has led him towards the moment when he will ask the question. As such, it is a ritual response. But more significantly it reflects his preparedness to enter into a new part of his life. With it he takes the final step on the road to fulfilment and the integration of his disunited self. In effect, the missing fragments of his soul have been returned to him, and at this moment he begins to function as a whole person, even as the Fisher King is healed and the land begins to flower. What greater gift could the Grail offer, and what could be more marvellous than Perceval's willingness to accept it!

This is the often painful journey which we must all undergo in some way. Whether men or women, these patterns are present in our lives from the day we are born. Many give up and fall by the wayside, slipping into patterns of self-abuse or abandonment to the pressures of the outer world. Many of us continue to seek the 'safe place' which is generally represented by our childhood home and the family circle. When we try to 'escape' from that place – as Perceval does – we are drawn back, inexorably, into our old habitual actions and ways of seeing and feeling. Often, this causes unnecessary pain and suffering to the new 'family' of friends, lovers and children which come to represent our original family. This is represented by Perceval's desire to become a knight – to become part of the family of the Round Table – and by his inability to see how he can do so. His desire is strong, but his intellectual understanding is weak. He tries, and sometimes succeeds through strength and intuition (which manifests blind, unthinking actions), but he fails in his main task until he has learned how to integrate feeling and action, masculine and feminine, and to recognize his own wounded state, at which point he is able to ask the question.

QUEST AND QUESTION

The asking of the question by the wounded person is of primary importance. For us the question might be, 'Why is this happening?', 'What does it mean?' or 'Why am I like this?' This one simple step triggers a response deep within the soul. It may be only the first step, but it is certainly the most important; once we have asked it, the process of healing can really begin.

But it is clear that the answers, which come from within each individual person, are less important than the asking. The Quest knights may set forth together, but they are soon separated, each going his own way; we too must find an individual answer to our own search, and this is reflected in the lives of many of us today. More and more people are experiencing a sense of isolation that seems to exclude friends and family, a feeling that we are somehow alone in a vast, unfriendly universe. We may seek any number of possible solutions to this kind of wound – orthodox religion, alternative spirituality, an endless quest for meaning and fulfilment.

The answer to this is to face the question of the wound of emptiness squarely, and to ask it what it means. This is the basis of the Grail Question, which is not just 'Whom does the Grail serve?', but 'What is the meaning of the wound, the cause of the pain?' And even more importantly, 'What is the cure?'

We need to make sense of what we see as needless, senseless suffering. Answers to all these questions can be found – but *only by asking* will we discover them. The exercise which follows is designed to enable you to ask, and to receive, answers. Here, as elsewhere throughout the visualizations in this book, pauses are inserted to give you time to access the necessary information from the meditations. In general these are meant to be in the region of a minute, though they can, of course, take longer.

Exercise 3 The Hermit

Spend some time considering the nature of the wounds you carry, their cause and when you first became aware of them. In the journey you are about to make you will be given an opportunity to ask questions about them, and to seek answers that will help you in your search for healing. Before you begin the meditation, be clear in your own mind about the questions you will ask and the reason for asking them. Then, when you are ready, enter into meditation, seeing before you the trunk of a great tree. You are close enough to see every grain and wrinkle of its ancient bark . . . then as you pull away you see that you are in a clearing in one of the great primeval forests which once clothed this land. On all sides mighty trees grow up towards the distant sunlight; beneath them all is dim and quiet. Looking around, you see a narrow, little used path that winds away amid the trees, and you decide to follow this wherever it leads . . . In a while you see a clearing ahead, and soon you enter it and stand looking round you. The sun strikes down and lights the place like a vast cathedral. But your eyes are drawn at once to a small round hut, of simple design, which stands to one side of the clearing. Next to it is an ancient stone, carved with curving and twining designs, and marked with the distinctive symbols of the ogam alphabet. Beside the stone, so still that you had failed to see him at first, is a figure in a plain brown robe. Seeing you approach, the figure looks up from the book he had been studying and rises to greet you. He seems like an elderly man, white haired and stooped, though still powerful, and his eyes are a bright and penetrating blue. He holds out his hand in welcome and speaks to you: 'I am the Hermit of these woods. How may I serve you?'

At once you are filled with a sense of focused energy, and with the desire to ask the all-important question concerning your state of woundedness and the healing you hope to find. You pour out your heart to the Hermit, who listens patiently, occasionally prompting you with gentle questions of his own. You never feel these are invasive or probing, and are thus encouraged to open yourself still further to his gentle perceptivity. . . [Pause]

When you have talked of all that you can, the Hermit takes your hand in his and holds it silently for a time. Then he speaks, giving you the benefit of his wisdom upon all that you have said. Listen and try to remember all that you hear, for you will want to write these things down when you are done. . . [Pause]

When he has finished speaking the Hermit blesses you by placing his hand upon your head. He then bids you goodbye and tells you that you may return there at any time you need, to ask of his wisdom and kindness. You give thanks for his words and prepare to depart, walking back through the mighty forest, which gradually fades around you, until you are back in the place from which you began. Take time to record the Hermit's words, and remember that you can return to visit him whenever you have need.

With this exercise you have taken another step on the road to healing the inner king and the inner kingdom. In the next chapter we shall begin to explore more deeply some of the mythic patterns which underlie not only this story but also the human dimension of our personal quest for healing.

3　The Family of the Grail

The Grail connects us with everything; the wound
separates us from everything
The Grail Castle K Johnson and M Elsbeth

THE WOUNDED FAMILY

It will be clear by now that several of the major players in the Grail story are related to each other. This can be shown by a family tree which derives from several sources. In considering the connections between these characters we begin to arrive at a geography of woundedness.

Virtually all the members of this extended family are wounded in some fashion or other. Perceval's mother is wounded by the death of her husband and sons, and by her refusal to accept

The Family of the Wounded King

the way of life which is laid down for all men of noble lineage in her time, to follow the way of chivalry and knighthood. Perceval is wounded by her over-protective nature and her desire to force him into a different mould. The Wounded King's hurts are catalogued in a number of different ways; he is unable to free himself, and is, in effect, a prisoner of woundedness. Garlon, whom we have yet to encounter, expresses his wounded nature in his attacks upon others. He represents the shadow side of the Wounded King's family. Dindraine, Perceval's sister, whom we shall meet again in Chapter 5, becomes wounded when she offers help to another; her wounds are thus significantly different from those of the others, and perhaps ultimately not wounds at all. Only the Grail Maiden and the Hermit cannot be said to possess wounds, though the former is perhaps wounded by her inability to act on behalf of her father. Each of these people represents an aspect of our own wounded state, and together they form an image with which we have become increasingly familiar over the last few years – that of the dysfunctional family, which we may call the Wounded Family in this context.

An increasing amount of evidence shows just how many wounds arise from familial situations. The Wounded Father, the Wounded Mother, the Wounded Child and the Wounded Brother/Sister form a recognizable community of woundedness, and many (if not all) their wounds arise from a degree of separation which has reached frightening proportions. Parents abuse their children, children reject their parents, siblings are bound into patterns of increasingly deadly rivalry, marriages and relationships break down and are blamed on the family, while the old notion of the family unit becomes increasingly hard to realize or accept. At a deeper level still, this reflects in the persons of the Wounded Female and the Wounded Male.

These are all trends which are increasing to such a degree that, if we do not do something to reverse them, we shall arrive at a point of stasis, with each individual locked away in his or her own state of woundedness, increasingly unable to respond to help or healing, and moving all the while towards a deeper degree of unconnectedness.

The problem also exists on a global scale. Countries are becoming increasingly assertive of their boundaries, their culture and ideology. At one extreme this is a reasonable assertion of cultural and racial identity; at the other it becomes a focus for 'racial purity' with the horrific results that we have seen in Bosnia. The wounds of culture, race and ideology are also evident, with an increasing number of internal expressions of this occurring as far apart as Ireland, Lebanon and Israel.

As we enter a new millennium in the West, and the more we talk in terms of a global village, it seems that this becomes less and less viable. Even electronic communications, much vaunted as a means of bringing people together, actually seem to isolate individuals as they spend longer hours chained to their computer terminals and less and less time in direct communicatio.1 with each other.

All these situations are manifestations of woundedness, and not all of them are easily accessed by those who seek to heal them. However, it is possible that if we learn about our own individual wounds, and how to heal them, we shall be working towards healing both personal and global family wounds.

That one story can help us to do this may seem far fetched, but by accessing the healing concepts contained within the texts we can at least take a step in the right direction as we move towards the inevitable changes that the future will bring. Every situation within our lives has its own story; by asking questions about the causes of that story, as we are prompted to do by working through the Grail story, we shall begin to perceive the nature of our own wounds and the possible ways in which they can be healed.

Throughout the remainder of this chapter, and beyond, we shall look more closely at some of the powerful mythological and symbolic characters and themes which illustrate the many aspects of woundedness which we can recognize. A more detailed list of these characters, with a brief breakdown of their qualities, will be found in Appendix 1.

The King Who Fishes for Health

We still know very little about the Fisher King himself. In all his incarnations he is first and foremost the guardian of a vessel possessing magical or wondrous properties. Usually, this is identified as the Grail, though other images occur. Beyond this we have learned little more than Chretien himself told us. We learn from later texts that he is one of a family of guardians whose task it is to keep the Grail safe against the day when someone will come who will achieve its mysteries.

A number of theories have been put forward over the years to explain the title 'Fisher King'. The most usual one is found within the texts which tell the early history of the Grail. Here we learn of an earlier Grail guardian, Bron or Hebron, whose name is reminiscent of the Celtic god Bran. He, according to the story, is given the task of feeding the company of disciples who follow Joseph of Arimathea. He does so with a single fish, emulating the feeding of the five thousand by Christ, and is thereafter called the Fisher King.

This reads like a medieval attempt to explain a title which was already obscure. A far more reasonable explanation stems from a misreading of the name *Le Roi Pescheur*, the Sinner King, as *Le Roi Pecheur*, the Fisher King. This fits in very well with the perceived nature of the guardian in the medieval romances with which we are dealing, where it is generally through some, often unstated, wrong that the king receives his wound.

In some instances the king is also called *Le Roi Mehaigne*, the Maimed King, a title which comes from a far older version of the story where physical damage to the king is related to the wounding of the land. As we shall see later this is an important aspect of the story. All we can practically say of him at this juncture is that in a certain sense he is fishing for his own lost soul-parts. The circumstances of his meeting with his nephew Perceval indicate that he is aware of the opportunity for healing, and that he seeks to encourage it as far as possible.

Chretien says simply that he is a king, and that he received his wound in battle. He tells us nothing about why the wound will not heal. We must therefore turn to the continuators of Chretien's text, who took up the strands of the story and elaborated it, to discover more of the nature of the king's wound, and some of the ways by which a cure may be found.

THE WOUND AND ITS CAUSES

The second and third continuations of *Perceval* add nothing significant to the nature and cause of the Fisher King's wound. In the third continuation, however, which is attributed to an otherwise unknown author named Wauchier, we learn that the wound was self-inflicted, not by the spear but by a mysterious sword which has featured throughout all the continuations as a kind of parallel to the Grail Quest. Both Perceval and Gawain at various times possess this weapon (or one so similar as to be the same) which either breaks at a crucial moment or is already broken and requires mending as further evidence of the hero's worthiness.

Much of the reason for its existence remains obscure until we reach Wauchier's continuation, where we see how easy it is to wound ourselves in a moment of anger or fear. We learn that the Fisher King had a brother named King Gon of Sert, who was treacherously killed by a knight named Partinial the Wild, who crept up behind him and split his skull with the sword, which then broke into several pieces. The Fisher King, who is relating this to Perceval on one of the latter's return visits to the Grail Castle, goes on:

> When they had washed and dressed him as finely as they could they laid him in a bier and brought him here to me, along with the sword . . . with which my brother had been killed. I gathered the pieces, which were brought to me by one of my nieces; she told me how it had wrought the death of her father, whom I loved so much, and assured me that if I kept the pieces until a knight came here and held the sword and made the pieces join again, then my brother . . . would be avenged by the one who repaired the sword. But I was so stricken with grief that I took the pieces . . . and immediately scythed through my thighs and severed every nerve, so that, without a lie, I've been helpless ever since, and always will be until I'm avenged. . . (14)

Perceval promises to carry out the righting of this wrong, and subsequently kills the treacherous Partinial and carries his head back to the Fisher King, who is immediately healed of his wound.

This theme of revenge is echoed in several of the retellings of the story, including a very crucial text known as *Peredur*. This version of the story, which is part of the collection of tales known as *The Mabinogion* (10), has been the cause of debate for a number of years. It is clearly very closely related to Chretien's version, following the shape and plot of the French poem throughout. Yet despite the fact that the manuscript tradition post-dates the composition of *Perceval*, it appears to retain an earlier and more primitive version of the story. It is likely that Chretien knew an earlier version of *Peredur*, possibly recited by a wandering story-teller, and that this formed the basis for his own account. However, the importance of the Celtic version lies in the variations which it offers.

Peredur's life and early adventures follow more or less the same lines as those of Perceval; however, when we get to the description of the Grail castle and the strange procession there are marked differences. Gone is the elaborate description of the procession with its beautiful maidens, rich candelabra and the mysterious vessel. Instead, as Perceval sits talking with his uncle (who is described as lame) he sees

> . . .*two lads entering the hall and then leaving as for a chamber: they carried a spear of incalculable size with three streams of blood running from the socket to the floor. When everyone saw the lads coming in this way they set up a crying and a lamentation that was not easy for anyone to bear, but the man did not interrupt his conversation with Peredur – he did not explain what this meant, nor did Peredur ask him. After a short silence two girls entered bearing a large platter with a man's head covered with blood on it, and everyone set up a crying and lamentation such that it was not easy to stay in the same house. (10)*

Later it transpires that the head belonged to Peredur's own cousin, who had been killed by the Nine Witches of Gloucester. With the help of Arthur and his warriors Peredur slays the hags, and is rewarded with the knowledge that he has avenged his family honour. But nothing more is explained: we learn no more about the bleeding spear, nor are there any references to the Waste Land or the Grail. There are other details which we shall look at later when we examine the various figures who assist Perceval in his quest. For the moment it is sufficient to note that in this version of the story the theme is one of vengeance rather than redemption, a fact which is not without significance in the matter of the wound and its causes.

THE NOBLE HEAD

The Celtic origins of much of the Grail symbolism are well known, and its study lies outside the range of this present work. However, it is worth looking at some of the analogues of the Wounded King story; and although the story in question is not a Grail romance as such, it casts some light on the story as a whole, and also contains some intriguing details.

The story itself is also from *The Mabinogion* (10), in fact from the Four Branches, a set of connected tales which are ostensibly non-Arthurian, though in fact a number of the characters reappear in later guises in the Arthurian corpus. The story of 'Branwen Daughter of Llyr' is a complex tale involving treachery and murder and a good deal of magic. Branwen, who is the sister of the huge god-like king Bran, is married to the king of Ireland. But once she has given him a son she is put aside and treated like a slave. She manages to send a message to her brother, however, who at once sets out for Ireland with an army. After prolonged fighting an uneasy peace is reached, but during the ensuing feast the Irish behave in a treacherous manner, attacking Bran and his men, who are unarmed. In the ensuing mêlée Bran is wounded by a poisoned spear, and as he does so calls out to his enemies to 'Beware of Morddwyd Tyllion'. This reference, which seems at first obscure, becomes clearer when it is realized that the name means 'The Pierced Thigh'. Bran is in fact referring to himself, and identifying himself as a type of Wounded King. Further evidence of the connection between Bran (who is later referred to as 'Bendegeid' or 'Blessed') and the Grail romances has long been recognized from the number of characters in the Arthurian mythos who bear the name Bran (or some variant of it), and by the similarity with the name of one of the most important Grail kings, Bron or Brons, which clearly derives from that of the Celtic figure.

A clue to a less often recognized aspect of the Grail Castle and its lord is also to be found in this text. After Bran's wounding he commands his followers to cut off his head, and to carry it with them to an island called Gwales. Here the disembodied head continues to address them, entertaining them with songs and stories, while the otherworldly Birds of Rhiannon sing to them, causing them to forget all the terrors of their ordinary life. This period lasts for 78 years, during which time the followers of Bran remain in a kind of suspended animation which, they are told, will continue as long as no one opens a certain door which looks towards the shore of Britain.

This period is known as 'The Entertainment of the Noble Head', and it parallels the visit of the hero to the Grail Castle in a number of details. The island with its feasting hall is a precursor of the Fisher King's hall, just as Bran is an early avatar of the Wounded King. In both places the opportunity exists to imbibe wisdom, and to find rest and healing. In both there is the suspension of time and death; neither Bran nor the Grail King can die. But the effects of this are very different. The Grail King awaits the coming of the one who will ask the question which will release him; Bran has forbidden his followers to take the one action which will cause his own death and end their time of recuperation.

Bran's entertainment of his followers, and the singing birds which cause them to forget the world, is not a bad thing in itself. The followers need rest and peace after the shock of battle and the wounding of their lord, but there is a negative aspect to this. The Entertainment of the Noble Head keeps them bound in a place which is so seductively delightful they are reluctant to leave, demonstrating how easily we can become prisoners of our wounds. In the story one of Bran's followers finally opens the forbidden door, driven to do so by the most human of urges – curiosity. When he does so all those on the island begin to remember their own wounds and sorrows, while the head of Bran begins to die. The long dream is over at this point, and they must deal with the issues of the outer world.

All this tells us that we cannot live *in* our wounds, or continue to give them power over us, without becoming more deeply wounded than before. We have to take the chance to break out, to make a fresh start. Of course this can be painful, and we may indeed be forced to remember our sorrows, but it is ultimately better to do this than to immure ourselves in a place where we cannot move forward. This, in its long-term effect, is as destructive and isolating as it is for the Grail King, held frozen by his painful wounds. It is ultimately as bad for us to be chained in a silken pavilion as in a stone cell.

This also touches upon the absolute singularity of purpose with which the Wounded King awaits the healing he *knows* will one day come. As one of the correspondents who answered the questionnaire movingly wrote: 'I wonder how many restless hours he spent in the undiverted agony of waiting. How many stars fell like tears in the long hours until dawn? How many dawns spread into the drear routine of another day? How many days closed into the sleepless prison of another night?' Healing does come in the end – not always after 78 years of waiting, but when the time is right. This is something we all need to consider when we ask for healing – *is it the right time to be healed*? This may sound strange, because we all want to be healed as quickly as possible. But there is an underlying idea, which drifts almost unnoticed through the story, that the king will be healed when the right day dawns, and not before. In other words sometimes we have to wait for healing because we still have something to learn from our wounds, and only when we have done so can we find a cure.

GRAIL KINGS AND ANTI-KINGS

The next important reference to the *cause* of the Wound is found in the version of the story composed by the medieval German writer Wolfram von Eschenbach. His *Parzival* (13), follows the same broad story-line as Chretien's, though Wolfram repeatedly mentions his disagreement with the French author's interpretation. *Parzival* contains many variations in the story, and extends it considerably with a vast structure of esoteric symbolism, much of it culled from Middle Eastern sources, brought back to Europe by returning Crusaders. Two prime points of difference between Wolfram and Chretien concern us here: the treatment of the Wound and its cause, and the addition of a 'negative' Grail guardian.

The Grail King's name is here given as Amfortas (sometimes interpreted as meaning 'man without power') and as a young man he greatly aspired to follow the way of chivalry and knightly pursuits. To the extent that, even after being 'called' to the Grail, as are all the family of guardians, he still sought to go forth in search of adventure, and took a lady to be his inspiration.

> As knight-errant the charming, comely youth won fame so exalted that he ran no risk of its being surpassed by any in all the lands of chivalry. His battle-cry was 'Amor!', yet that shout is not quite right for humility. (13)

One day this noble youth set forth in search of adventure and encountered a pagan knight, who himself aspired to win the Grail. They fought, and Amfortas slew his opponent, but not before the latter had wounded him with a spear which entered his body through the scrotum. When he returned home in agony, the knight's friends and family did everything in their power to find healing for him, but despite a vast array of cures, he remained in perpetual pain, 'too ill to live, but unable to die'. Later a prophecy is made that he will only be healed when the destined person comes and asks the question concerning the Grail.

Here, then, the cause of the Wound is perhaps pride, though Wolfram's text is by no means clear on the matter. Amfortas rides out under the banner of Love (amor), but turns it to 'war' when he encounters the pagan knight. This is an aspect of the story to which Robert Johnson has rightly drawn attention as an outward manifestation of the human inclination towards aggression rather than acceptance. Not only does Amfortas choose to follow the way of chivalry, after having been chosen to be one of the destined guardians of the Grail, but he seems to be unable to accept the idea of another – especially a pagan – seeking the sacred object. He is both more concerned with wordly matters, and perceives his service to his lady as more important than his service to the Grail. In this he is like many people who are called to a higher task but who turn away and become more deeply involved in worldly matters in an endeavour to forget their true course through life.

Wolfram adds a further level of complexity to the plot by introducing a kind of Anti-Grail King named Clingsor. This man is perceived as totally negative, determined to acquire the Grail for personal aggrandisement. To him the Grail is power, and he believes that once he possesses it he can manipulate its power for himself. In a mocking parody of the Grail King, Wolfram makes Clingsor a black magician and gives him a wound – he is castrated by a knight who discovers him in bed with his wife. Because of this Clingsor hates all men and women, and uses his power only for evil. He possesses a great castle which is filled with dark magic in mocking shadow of the Grail Castle. In Wagner's 19th-century version of the story, the opera *Parzival*, this is taken a step further. Clingsor castrates himself in a desire to emulate the Wounded King, perceiving the Wound as power and himself as a worthy successor to Amfortas. In this he represents all those who utilize their wounds to give them the illusion of strength and power, who trade off their wounds to elicit pity from others, or who are wounded by their desire to control everything and everyone around them. Such actions are both self-deluding and disempowering. Those who adopt this method of dealing with their wounds inevitably end up realizing the hollowness of their lives, which essentially revolve around a negative set of values and a false understanding of their woundedness.

THE SAVAGE KNIGHT

Following the development of the Grail myth it is interesting to see the changes that occur in the episodes concerning the Wounded King. We have seen how the later versions introduced a negative Anti-Grail figure. In the great compilations of stories which followed on from Chretien and Wolfram, there is an increasing emphasis on the theological interpretation of the story. Once the Grail has become identified with the Cup of the Last Supper and the symbolism of the Eucharist, the causes of the Wound and their cure are made to reflect man's fallen state. Thus the Grail King's wound – perceived as a salutary lesson which must be endured in order to learn from it – is inflicted by an angel, and the healing of both king and land is revealed through the power and love of Christ.

This is of course a perfectly valid interpretation, and one which, for those who adhere to the path of Christianity, works well. But this book is addressed primarily at those who have a spiritual rather than a religious outlook, or who may even be seeking to heal the wounds which can spring from following a religious path too closely. Nevertheless it is within these vast and rambling theological edifices that we find one of the most significant additions to the story. The episode in question is best represented in Le Morte Darthur (12) of Sir Thomas Malory, written in the 15th century and thus one of the latest of the medieval romances to deal with Arthurian material. In fact Malory was working from texts like The Lancelot-Grail (9), a 13th-century compilation assembled by monks of the Cistercian order which is possibly the most Christianized version of all. But Malory was no mere translator. He adapted the works radically, altering and cutting wherever he saw fit, and in the process created a masterpiece of English prose which may still be read with pleasure more than five hundred years after it first appeared in print. The additions which it makes to the story of the Fisher King are of considerable importance, and worth giving in some detail.

Having told the story of Arthur's conception, birth and early deeds, Malory proceeds to the founding of the Round Table and the early adventures of its knights. One of these is named Balin le Sauvage, a knight of Northumbria who is famed for his quick temper and inclination to pick a fight. As the story opens he has just been released from prison, where he had languished for slaying one of the King's cousins. However, when one of the Ladies of the Lake appears, carrying a sword which no one can draw from its scabbard, Balin steps forward and is successful. He then embarks on a series of adventures which culminate in a tragic end. Before this, however, events take place which are to have a far-reaching effect upon the entire Arthurian world.

Dispatched by the king to bring back a certain knight to the court, Balin sees his charge killed before his eyes by an invisible adversary, named by the dying knight as Garlon. Balin determines to discover this evil fellow and to exact just revenge upon him. He takes with him the haft of the spear which had killed the first knight. Along the way he falls in with another man, who is likewise slain by the invisible attacker, and soon after that he meets with a nobleman who complains to him that his son had been wounded by an invisible knight, the brother of a king named Pellam who lives close by. Only the blood of this invisible knight can cure the wounded youth. Balin at once sets forth and soon arrives at Pellam's castle. There he is made welcome and begins to ask about the knight named Garlon, who is pointed out to him as a man with a dark face. Balin considers what is best to do, for he fears that if he attempts to slay the evil man he might not escape with his own life; whereas if he waits he might never have a better opportunity.

As he watches Garlon becomes aware of him, and at once comes over and strikes him in the face for staring. Without further debate Balin draws his sword and slays Garlon with a single blow. Then he takes the haft of the spear which had killed the knight in his charge and drives it into the dead man's body, crying out that now there is enough blood for the nobleman to heal his son.

Uproar breaks out and King Pellam himself catches up a grim weapon and cries out that no one save he should attack the knight who had slain his brother. Balin defends himself, but his sword breaks in pieces. What happens next is best told in Malory's words (15):

> And when Balin was weaponless he ran into a chamber for to seek some weapon, and so from chamber to chamber, and no weapon he could find, and always King Pellam after him. And at last he entered into a chamber that was marvellously well decorated. . . and a bed arrayed with a cloth of gold, the richest that might be thought, and one lying therein, and thereby

stood a table of clean gold with four pillars of silver that bare up the table, and upon the table stood a marvellous spear strangely wrought. And when Balin saw the spear, he gat it in his hand and turned him to King Pellam, and smote him passingly sore with the spear, that King Pellam fell down in a swoon, and therewith the castle roof and walls brake and fell to the earth, and Balin fell down so that he might not stir foot nor hand. And so the most part of the castle, that was fallen down through that dolorous stroke, lay upon Pellam and Balin three days. (Book 11, Chapter XV)

Merlin comes at the end of the three days and frees Balin from the ruins of the castle. At this point we learn that this was in fact the Castle of the Grail, that King Pellam is its guardian, and that the figure lying in the bed was that of Joseph of Arimathea, who was responsible for bringing both the Grail and the Spear (the latter being the Lance of Longinus, which had been used to give the death blow to Christ on the cross) to Britain. The effects of this 'Dolorous Blow' are to be terrible. The land all around the castle is laid waste, and the king himself will remain wounded but undying until one shall come who can heal him.

As he rides away, Balin sees death on every side, while those who have survived curse him and predict his death. Shortly after he hears a hunting horn blowing the 'mort', the death of the huntsman's prize, and Balin knows that it is blown for him. Arriving at an island where the custom is for all comers to meet the defender of the place, Balin accepts the challenge along with an offer of fresh arms and armour, since his own were lost in the ruins of Pellam's castle. Thus anonymous he fights and kills the defender of the island, receiving his own death wound in the process. As he breathes his last he discovers that his opponent is his own brother, Balan. Merlin comes and buries them side by side in a single grave, and taking the pommel from Balin's sword, sets it in a new weapon. He then places this into a block of red marble and leaves it to float miraculously in the waters of a river. Later, it is to float downstream to Camelot, where Galahad, the destined Grail winner, who supersedes Perceval in the latter romances, finds and wields it in his own quest.

This remarkable story, told in Malory's terse prose, is perhaps the most significant addition to the story we have met since Chretien's tale of *Perceval*, bringing in as it does the sinister figure of Garlon – related, as we shall see, to both Clingsor and another adversarial figure, Amangons, and providing the most convincing scenario yet for the wounding of the king.

The Child of the Grail

In this same text we learn more about the Grail Princess, Pellam's daughter, who in virtually all the stories is represented as a rather static figure. Yet she is considered sufficiently worthy to be the bearer of the Grail, as it is she who carries the sacred vessel in the procession of the Hallows. In most of the texts she remains a somewhat shadowy figure, but in the cycle of stories from which Malory was working, she attains a new prominence as the mother of Galahad.

Pellam, the name given to the Wounded King in Malory's book, has a daughter named Elaine, who has been mysteriously enclosed in a tower room for five years. She is forced to sit in a cauldron of boiling water, until the coming of a knight brave enough to set her free. Several knights, including Sir Gawain, have tried but failed, but Lancelot, the supreme hero of the Round Table, successfully braves his way into the tower and brings out the lady. Elaine is unharmed by her ordeal and Lancelot is clearly attracted to her, though his love for Guinevere prevents him from anything more than this. Pellam, however, has other ideas. A prophecy has been made that his daughter will bear a child by the best knight in the world (a title generally applied to Lancelot), and that this child will successfully bring about the healing of the Dolorous Blow and the Waste Land. Pellam therefore sets out to bring about a liaison between Lancelot and Elaine. He employs the services of a woman versed in magic to give Lancelot a potion which will give him the illusion he is with Guinevere. He then sends him a message, with a ring which had been given to Lancelot by the Queen, inviting him to meet her at a small castle close by the house of the Grail. Drugged and bemused, Lancelot sleeps with Elaine and begets a child upon her. This will be the saintly Galahad, who will outstrip all others in pursuit of the Grail.

There are a number of interesting points in this story. The Wounded King is shown to be taking action on his own behalf to bring about the eventual healing of his wounds. We are not told whether Elaine is a willing player in the plot to ensnare

Lancelot, though she is clearly attracted to him too. Further-more, although we are told that her imprisonment in the vat of boiling water was at the behest of Morgan le Fay, who was jealous of her beauty, there is an underlying suggestion that her suffering is a mirror of her father's wounded state, and therefore part of the effects of the Dolorous Blow. In any case, both are in effect the prisoners of their wounds and must make an individual effort to find healing. If this is a correct interpreta-tion of the story we must also understand that the opportunity for Elaine's release from her pain is already available, and that she may well be aware of this, just as Pellam knows that he will ultimately be healed by his own grandson. This is part of an underlying theme which runs through all of the stories concern-ing the Wounded King – that healing is a natural concomitant of woundedness, and that the promise of the cure is contained within the causality of the wound.

Although we seldom hear of Elaine again in this story, she does make a significant appearance in a later version, *Diu Crone* by Heinrich von dem Tulin (3), in which her role is similar to that of the Hideous Damsel, warning Gawain of the need to ask the question when next he sees her – a direction which, when he remembers it, causes him to become a successful Grail winner (see Chapter 5).

Elaine is thus both a guide and helper in these stories, func-tioning as a prompter who helps both the Wounded King and his ultimate healer to fulfil their tasks. In the terms of our own journey towards healing we may see her as representing the inner impulse to seek answers to the questions which promote health: 'Why am I wounded? Why must this be? What can I do to find healing?'

THE SPEAR THAT WOUNDS AND HEALS

All wounds have their causes, and we have seen some of the reasons for our own. The Fisher King's Wound is generally caused by a spear, and this weapon also features extensively in the literature of the Grail and its Celtic precursors. A closer examination of the various texts in which this appears, and of the themes which are associated with it, reveal some interesting facts both about the nature of the Wound and its potential cure.

The spear is a device intended to pierce the flesh and cause a wound. Yet in the Grail romances it also figures as a source of healing. Specifically, the spear which causes the wound can also heal the wound; or, in terms of our present discussion, that which causes the Wound can also heal the Wound. This probably relates in part at least to an ancient belief that the blood of the person doing the wounding can heal the wounds of the person he has attacked. This is very much a part of the reasoning behind the Welsh story of *Peredur* (10), which is, as we have seen, a vengeance tale in which blood plays an important part. Whether the reasoning originally was that to spill the blood of one's adversary, or of the person who had slain a friend or relative, was more than a simple act of vengeance, cannot be said with any degree of certainty. But in the Grail myths it is without doubt very much more. This is possibly due to the Christian influence which profoundly altered the shape of the original stories. The mystery of the Eucharist, which presents spiritual healing through sanctified bread and wine, is perfectly in line with the idea of the Grail as a healing vessel, which is perhaps why so many of the later stories of the Grail's physical manifestation perceive it as a miraculous source of health.

Chretien de Troyes referred to the spear as '*la lance qui saigne*' – the lance that heals – an idea which connects it with a long-standing tradition of the need to seek the cause of a wound in order to discover the cure. This forms the basis of all complementary medicine, such as homeopathy, which treats an illness by submitting it to a minute dosage of a substance which might be considered as an underlying cause of the problem. In a similar way, certain types of snake bite are treated with venom to counter their effects.

In classical mythology, when the wounded hero Telephos visits the temple of Apollo and asks for healing for his wounds, the oracle answers 'that which wounds will also heal!' He sets out to find Achilles, who had wounded him in the siege of Troy. Only the hero could heal the wounds he had caused, just as only the object which had caused the wound, wielded by the right person, could bring an end to the Wounded King's sufferings.

It has been frequently pointed out that the spear featured in the Grail myths can be seen to derive much of its nature from the fiery spear of the Celtic god Lugh, or indeed to its numerous variants which appear in Celtic tradition in a wide variety of forms – from spears that burn to spears that bleed – and which have to be doused in cauldrons containing blood, water or poison. It is worth noting here also that one such spear belongs to the Irish god of healing and medicine, Dian Cecht; while Lugh himself, though a warlike deity, is also often associated with healing wells. This ambiguous aspect of the spear is very much a part of the way in which the Wounded King may find healing – by looking to the cause of his pain and suffering and seeking to transcend both the Wound and its origin.

Friedman Wieland, in his book *The Journey of the Hero* (60), points out that wounds must often be re-lived and re-experienced in order to find a cure, particularly in the case of childhood wounds, where the sufferer was often unaware of the nature of the hurt and must be helped to understand it. Wieland, who is a Jungian analyst, then remarks:

> When a person opens up to the unfelt hurt from childhood and becomes conscious of it, his wounds can bleed. The process of life that had stagnated in chronic conditions can then flow again, and the wounds can heal. Faced with suffering, Parzival had remained an observer. As the king's suffering was to continue in stagnation, his journey too had become a journey of suffering. The king's wound and the starving of the land had now become his own wound.

Old wounds must sometimes be re-opened, otherwise they may turn bad, and the sufferer remain in a static state, just as the Fisher King does. If this is carried out in a state of awareness and preparedness, the results are healing rather than the cause of further suffering. However, there is a destructive side to the therapeutic practice, advocated by many therapists, of digging over the trauma that caused the wound. This method *can* be both unhealing and unrestorative, but any pain generated by this experience comes from our being unprepared for what comes next. In the exercise which follows you will be given the opportunity to re-live an old wound, but in a safe environment where you are nurtured and protected. This visualization ends in sleep, and on this occasion you need not consciously return by awakening to your normal surroundings. Simply follow the journey into sleep, from which you may awaken in your own time.

Exercise 4 The Grail Wound

Close your eyes and prepare to embark upon a journey. As you allow your senses to adjust to the movement from outer to inner consciousness, become aware that you are standing once again before the entrance to the Castle of the Grail. This time there is no need to cross the Sword-Bridge, which lies behind you, and there, waiting to welcome you, is the now familiar figure of the Hermit, who bids you follow him. . .

This time, as you enter the hall, you see that many people are already seated at the long tables which stretch down either side of the room. But the Hermit leads you straightaway into a side chamber, where the buzz of conversation from the hall is at once silenced, and where a cool and peaceful atmosphere surrounds you. Set beneath a window, through which you can see the branches of a great tree stirring gently in the breeze, is a low couch. The Hermit indicates that you should take your ease upon it, and to await the coming of the one you have come there to see. . .

The Hermit departs, and for a brief time you are alone. You realize that this is the first time you have been thus, in the Castle of the Grail, and you wonder greatly that you are so close to the mystery. Spend a few moments considering this, and then call to mind some deep and long-established wound that troubles you. Be unstinting in this, and do not hold back from recognizing the reality of this hurt. Though the summoning of this wound may well be painful, remember that you are in the place where ultimately you may find healing for all of the wounds that you bear within. Take as long as you need to do this . . .[Pause]

When you have spent some time in this way, become aware that someone has entered the room and is standing patiently by your side. You look up and see the most kindly face you have ever seen, marked with lines of compassion and selfless love. The person may be male or female, old or young, but above all they possess the essence of care and wisdom. This, you know at once, is a Healer, someone to whom you can pour out your heart, who has heard everything and anything there is to hear, no matter how terrible or seemingly insignificant it may be. And this is just what you now do, putting into words all the fear and terror and pain, the loneliness, rejection and unconnectedness that is in your life. Take your time in this and, as before, be as unstintingly honest as you can be, knowing that no one else will ever hear what you say unless you wish it. . . [Pause].

When you have said all that you need to say, the Healer gently takes both your hands, and looking far off into the distance beyond you, begins to sing. The song is ancient and beautiful, full of unexpected cadences and changes of key. The Healer's voice is rich and vibrant, full of the same overwhelming sensitivity that is reflected in his or her face. It is like nothing you have heard or experienced before, and as you listen you become aware that it is having a deep and profound effect upon you. Take your time to consider this effect while you listen to the sweet harmonies of the song. . . [Pause]

In time – who can say how long, for in this place there is no such dimension – you hear that the song has ended. You look again at the Healer, whose eyes are still closed, and realize that something has passed from you to her or him. Some ancient, deep-seated hurt has been changed, softened, healed in a way you could not have imagined. You try to utter your thanks, but the Healer merely shakes his or her head and places a finger against your lips. Then, as quietly as she or he entered, he or she is gone, leaving you alone again in the bright room with the sound of the breeze in the tree outside the window, lulling you into a gentle sleep. . .

From this sleep you will awaken in time to your normal consciousness, the images you have seen fading into sleep, and sleep itself leading in time to a quiet awakening.

THE GATES OF THE WOUND

It is a curious paradox that under certain circumstances our wounds can actually help us to find the cause of their healing. Joseph Nagy, who is the foremost expert on the myths relating to the Irish hero Fionn macCumhail, sees the magical spear as a means of gaining access to and knowledge of the Otherworld, as 'an instrument for opening the. . . [Otherworld]' and which can also 'enter. . . the supernatural realm' (47). If he is correct then the spear of the Grail cycle, to which it is so closely related, may also be recognized as opening the way between the worlds. This is, of course, very much at the heart of the mystery which makes the shaman a 'wounded healer' – not because he or she has to undergo sickness and wounding to be able to heal the wounds of others, but because this suffering opens up the ways between the worlds, just as they do in the Fionn stories and in those of various Arthurian heroes.

This is not an easy concept to work with. We are used to regarding our wounds as adversarial to our inner health, and it is difficult to accept the idea that they might actually help us (other than in the way that we hang on to certain wounds for the wrong reasons). Seen from this perspective it is possible to read the story of Perceval's journey as an experience designed to initiate him into a recognition of his wounds and as a way of expiating childhood fears and fantasies. As we saw in the story of Bran, sometimes we have to wait for the right time to heal. It is even possible to view the whole Wounded King story as part of a cycle of wounding and healing which exists to help those who are already suffering to progress. Thus the King can be seen as someone whose life has become static; in the Balin story he remains quiescent of Garlon's deeds, until challenged and awoken by the death of his dark brother. Yet he has the ability to fish for a healer, to pull forth healing for himself from the waters of the Wound. For though the Waste Land is without water, there is still a moat around the castle, and it is in these waters, which form a barrier between the would-be Grail-seeker and his goal, that the King finds ease from his suffering.

As Robert Bly has wisely remarked, drawing on the imagery of the Wounded King:

> Religion . . . does not mean doctrine, or piety, or purity, or 'faith', or 'belief', or my life given to God. It means a willingness to be a fish in the holy water, to be fished for . . . to bow the head and take hints from one's dreams, . . . to eat grief as the fish gulps water and lives. It means being both fisherman and fish, not to be the wound but to take hold of the wound. Being a fish is to be active; not with cars or footballs, but with soul. (18)

The kind of experience in which we either do not know that we are wounded, or else know it and do nothing, is part of a process by which we are prompted to seek healing, either in a direct fashion like the Wounded King himself, or in the less focused journey that Perceval undertakes – still driven by a need to explore his sense of detachment, but without any real sense of where he is headed or what he will encounter. Breaking through this barrier is part of the process of healing. The next exercise is designed to help you to find the way past your wounds into a safe and tranquil harbour where you may find rest and healing for your tired soul.

Exercise 5 The Way Between the Worlds

Prepare to set out on a journey . . . from this world . . . to the Otherworld . . . through the doors of inner perception . . . on the waters of dream. . . Become aware that you are standing by the edge of a wide stretch of water. It is night, and a round moon rises over the scene, casting a bright glow over everything. By its light you see coming towards you across the water a small craft in which is a single figure. As the boat grounds against the shore the figure looks up at you and you see that it is an old woman, whose eyes are sunken in her head, and whose arms, as they rest on the pole which she has been using to propel the boat, seem too frail to pilot even this small craft.

'So, you have come at last,' she says. 'Are you ready to depart?'

'Where shall I go?' you ask.

'To the Island of Healing Dreams, of course,' she answers.

'Then I am ready,' you say.

'What payment do you offer?' demands the crone.

'I have none,' you reply.

'Then you shall not go.'

'What payment can I offer?' you ask.

'You must admit to a wound and tell everything concerning it,' replies the old one.

At this you hesitate, but you know in your heart that you must do this. Search, therefore, for a wound of which you have more knowledge, or which pains you most deeply, and tell her everything you can. . . [Pause].

When you are done the old woman nods, and bids you step into her boat. She then poles you out across the moonlit waters until you reach the shore of a low-lying island. Even before you reach it you can smell a wonderful variety of scents, wafted to you upon the wind. . . The smell of night-blooming flowers . . . of wood-smoke, and the simmer of rich foods. By the time you step ashore you are eager for whatever lies ahead. . .

You walk inland a short distance until you see a fire burning in a sheltered spot. As you approach you see a figure tending a large fish suspended above the crackling flames. He looks up as you approach and you see that it is an old man whose eyes are as merry as the new day. He greets you warmly and invites you to join him. You sit by his side, enjoying the warmth of the fire and the smell of the roasting fish. . .

Soon the feast is ready, and the old man, smiling but unspeaking, offers you some of the fine white flesh, and clear fresh water like wine to wash it down. You eat hungrily, and are quickly replete. The food tastes better than anything you can ever remember eating, and when you have finished you lie back comfortably, basking in the warm glow of the fire. . .

Almost before you realize it you are asleep and dreaming. . . or perhaps you are dreaming awake. . . but there comes to you a vision of your own life and of the wounds you have gained on your journey, and out of this something else. . . a healing that is as unexpected as it is joyful. . . Take your time to experience it fully. . . [Pause]

Some time later you find yourself still beside the fire. The old man has gone, and now the old woman sits there, waiting patiently for you to notice her. When she sees that you are awake, she beckons you to follow her, and leads the way back to the shore and the waiting boat. You are sorry to leave this peaceful place, but knowing that you may return there whenever you have need, you allow the old woman to pole you back to the shore where you first entered this place. . .

You bid farewell to the old woman, who smiles at you now, and waves you on your way. . . You awaken slowly to your normal surroundings, and write down all that you saw and experienced on the Island of Healing Dreams.

THE WOUNDS OF THE BLOOD

In Balin's story the cause of the Wound is described as vengeance, but there is more to it than that. There is indeed something of a fateful quality about the whole story. Balin acts, after all, in good faith according to the mores of the time. He seeks first of all to avenge the treacherously slain knights whom he encounters along the way; lastly he seeks to provide the blood which will heal the wounded boy, an aspect of the story which is often overlooked, but which is not without significance. Nor is he aware that in seizing the spear he is using a sacred relic to defend himself. The outcome is the same anyway: the land is laid waste and King Pellam receives a wound that will only be healed by the right person at the right time.

The idea that the blood of the attacker can also heal the wounds he or she has caused is touched upon several times in the Grail stories. This, as previously noted, is possibly a natural outcome of the underlying Christian symbolism which has become attached to the Grail in the later stories, and with the concept of sacred blood in more ancient cultures. (In our own time we have become distressingly aware of the idea of poisoned blood through the AIDS crisis; the Grail story represents blood as a healing agent.) It also suggests that those who are wounded have *within themselves* the ability to heal.

In the 13th-century Grail text known as *Perlesvaus* (15), King Arthur is the subject of an episode in which a burning spear is quenched by his own blood. Here he is attacked by a Black Knight:

> The head of the lance was huge, and it burned with a great flame, sinister and terrifying, which reached right down to the knight's hand. . . [He] smote the king on the boss of his shield; the burning blade pierced the wood, rent the sleeve of his hauberk and tore into his arm: the king felt the burning of the wound and was filled with rage, while the knight drew out his lance and rejoiced in his heart to see the king wounded. But the king in his dismay was astonished to see that the knight's lance was no longer burning. (15)

The Black Knight subsequently admits that his lance could only be quenched with the king's blood, an important detail in this complex of imagery surrounding the Wound. Though he begs for mercy, the king is so angry that he slays him, then watches as his body is dismembered by invisible hands and carried off piece by piece. Arthur is then informed that only the Black Knight's blood can heal the wound caused by the burning spear, an interesting analogue which suggests even more strongly that Arthur was himself at one time seen as the Wounded King; this further clarifies the Grail story, since it is to seek healing for king and land that Arthur sends the Round Table knights forth in search of their goal.

Arthur's wound is here said to be in his arm rather than his thigh, and his reaction is one of anger. He cannot recognize the wound for what it is, a ritual blow which could open the way for him: a common reaction among those who experience wounding. The wound is a thing to be feared and hated, rather than embraced and worked with. It is this which causes so many wounded people to stay wounded; if they could only recognize the power of the Wound to transcend ordinary reality, they would find not only healing but also access to their own inner power.

The persistent presence of the vengeance theme at the heart of some versions of the story is a painful one. We live in a world where vengeance, whether through terrorism or organized crime, features very largely. Even in our personal lives we are lucky if we avoid encountering vengeance at least once. Of course, we are all aware that this is wrong. What, then, are we to make of such episodes as that in which Balin kills Garlon? Is it enough to say that he was evil and deserved to die? Or are we merely preserving the old 'eye for an eye' mentality?

Essentially, the myth transcends such concerns, being more concerned with balance and polarization. Thus the existence of Garlon balances the existence of the Grail King who is his brother, and the presence of Clingsor and his followers balance the presence of Arthur and the Round Table Knights. And the actions of Balin, though perceived as negative, in fact spark off the whole cycle of healing. There is a sense that our wounds, like those of the King, exist to teach us something. This is not to advocate the idea of 'learning through suffering', but merely to point out that the actions of everyone concerned in the myth, whether they are perceived as positive or negative, are part of a greater whole. No one likes to see suffering, whether it is of an individual or a nation, but occasionally we may see a good coming out of this.

At another level, behind the idea of blood and sacrifice, lies the notion of Ancestral healing. In this we witness a cleansing of patterns which may occur again and again within our own family, or on a larger scale in the history of the world. One only has to look at the current troubles in Ireland, or the boiling over of the Balkan states, and then look at their history to see how this can occur. Old patterns *do* repeat themselves, and the only way to heal these kinds of wounds are by acknowledging them and taking responsibility for our own ancestral history. This is implicit within all the sources we are exploring, especially those which deal with the links between the Wounded King and the Waste Land. There we can see old patterns working themselves out, but always with the promise of healing. Even when the people of the Fisher King's court are so distraught that they spend time every day bemoaning their fate and sorrowing the wounds of king and land, they are aware that the healing agent will one day appear. It is that hope which transcends the vengeance quest, and turns it into a healing story represented in the idea of the blood of the abuser being also the agent of healing for the abused. In the next exercise we shall encounter this idea directly as we make a shamanic journey to meet Balin le Sauvage.

Exercise 6 Balin's Journey

In this exercise you will be making a journey to the Underworld, the place of the ancestors, to meet the knight who slew Garlon and who struck the Dolorous Blow. He should not be perceived as a negative character, but as someone caught up in the pattern of the developing Grail myth. His knowledge and understanding of both the causes of the woundedness and the nature of ancestral healing are great. (Remember that he and his brother accidentally slew each other.) The purpose of the journey is to ask for information and healing for any ancestral wounds you possess. Have this thought in mind as you prepare to ask the Questing Beast to accompany you as always, and to take you to meet Balin. Engage with him in dialogue, and try to remember all that you are told. This particular journey may well prove disturbing, since it is bound to throw up any inherited causes of woundedness, some of which you may already be aware of, but others which may well prove surprising or shocking. At the end be sure to close down carefully with food and drink and if necessary take a walk in the outside air to clear away any lingering thoughts.

THE FOOL'S QUESTION

These are some of the characters and situations encountered by those who undertake the quest for healing. Each of them impinges in some way upon the seeker, helping or hindering their cause. Yet no matter what experiences we receive – both positive and negative – we are still exploring the realm of wonder at the heart of creation, where the most important action is to *ask questions*.

In the myth the all-important question is asked by a simple fool, Perceval, whose name may mean 'pierce the vale', and who sets free the waters (of emotion, of the soul) which have been frozen by the inability of the Wounded King to act. Others must act in his stead – or, one might say, his own child (his feminine side!) or his simple self, which owns no high intellectual dimension, must begin to act for him – enacting the healing which will come from within. As Robert Johnson points out in his *Fisher King and the Handless Maiden* (25), Perceval is only required to *ask* the question, not to answer it! The question is that which connects, and the answer (or answers) emerge from the events which then take place.

The implication of the story is that the Grail Procession takes place *every day*, and that in the same way healing is available to us at every moment; we have only to take charge and *ask for help* to receive healing. Failure to do this is as crucial as failing to ask the Grail question. When Perceval sees the Grail borne through the Fisher King's hall he is seeing an everyday miracle. When we perceive the inner ability to heal our own wounds we are perceiving the daily wonder of our own lives. The path of the Grail Hero – who represents every one of us – is littered with signs and wonders, extraordinary events used to illuminate everyday events, in order that we might see the extraordinary power and beauty of the living world. The Grail is essentially always present; we simply cannot see it. It appears in flashes of profound insight, in moments in which we transcend our ordinary consciousness. Those glimpses are the motivation to go further.

Of course these answers are not always easy ones. Often there will be problems to overcome and dangers to face along the way. Just as the Quest Knights meet opposition of every kind, so too will we find our steps dogged with setbacks and pitfalls. Thus, in many of the versions of the Grail story the way into the castle is via a gate, or gates, which make entry difficult and which require a special degree of courage to surmount them.

One is by the Water Gate, which necessitates passing *beneath* the water. It is usually taken by Gawain, which fits entirely with his character. The other method of entrance is via the Sword Bridge, a perilously narrow way which is as sharp as a sword (indeed, it is often depicted literally as a sword in the medieval illustrations which accompany these stories). The hero sometimes has to crawl across it, cutting hands, knees and feet in the process. Few are successful. It represents the crossing over from an outer to an inner perception, from a state of blind woundedness to a state in which we are able to recognize our wounds and seek healing. When Perceval crosses the drawbridge leading to the Grail Castle he is moving from an outer world-view to an inner one. He must integrate the experience of his outer state of being with what he encounters within the castle; he cannot do this yet, hence the fact that he must leave the castle by the way he entered, the drawbridge, which closes behind him, cutting him off from the inner state which he needs to understand before he can find the courage to ask the question.

In the mystical world of the Grail space becomes time and distances travelled represent symbolic states of mind and being. One must be wary of becoming lost in these inner places, for though we can learn much from walking there, we should never forget that the wisdom we acquire in the inner worlds needs to be integrated and applied in the outer. We cannot run away from ourselves in this way, or abdicate our humanity in favour of Otherworldly life. It is in the *blending* of these two kinds of experience that our spiritual, emotional and physical healing takes place. We must journey to the Grail Castle, cross the Sword Bridge or pass through the Water Gate, face the opponents that await us – but it is what we *bring back* from the journey, and what we do with it, that is vital for the healing, not only of ourselves but of the land as well (see Chapter 4).

Perceval encounters another fearsome bridge in the second continuation of Chretien's poem. In this instance the bridge becomes a means of indicating the rightful hero. Perceval is riding to a tournament with another knight when they reach a bridge which has been partially built by an Otherworldly woman. When her lover was killed she refused to complete the bridge and declared that only the best knight in the world would be able to cross it. As Perceval rides onto the half-completed structure, it wrenches itself away from the bank and swings around so that the end on which he stands is now attached to the further bank. His companion is left behind and declares that Perceval must indeed be the best knight in the world to have accomplished this test.

Here is a scenario which we may all recognize from our own life experience. How many times have we set out to reach a certain goal, only to find that we have, literally, run out of road? Dreams built upon others' dreams may have this effect also. But in each case we have the ability to change the situation; we can turn the bridge and cross in safety if we wish. The following visualization is intended to help us do just that.

Exercise 7 The Perilous Bridge

Close your eyes and prepare to enter into meditation. As you allow your surroundings to fade become aware that you are standing on a dusty roadway that leads towards a great medieval castle. The walls are tall and white, reflecting the sun. Brightly coloured banners flutter over the walls, and from the topmost tower flies the image of a golden Grail against a background of red. The road is deserted, though you can tell from its well-trodden appearance that many feet have walked there before. This, you realize, must be one of the many ways to the Castle of the Grail. Filled with awe and wonder you set out on this road, following it to the very walls of the castle. There you are brought to a halt, for though you can see the mighty gates, there is a deep moat, filled with water, between them and you, and there seems no way to get across. Then, as you stand uncertainly in the shadow of the great walls, you see that a slender bridge spans the moat – but a bridge such as you have never seen before. Slender as a sword it stretches before you, its surface rough and jagged. This seems like the only way to cross to the Castle of the Grail, but your whole soul rebels against the idea. Surely this is too great a task for you. You imagine the rough stones tearing at your flesh, until you can almost feel the pain and see your blood running down the sides of the bridge . . . Then, seemingly from within the castle, comes a voice, that whispers in your ear: 'You *must* cross if you are to find the healing you seek.'

Filled with trepidation you approach the beginning of the bridge. It stretches before you, seeming almost endless. But on the far side is a gentle green bank, and above that the gates which open inwards upon the mystery of the Grail. Summoning all your courage you prepare to cross the bridge, thinking as you do of the wounds for which you have come here to find healing. There are two choices before you. One is to cross on hands and knees, the other is to try to walk across the narrow span of the bridge. The sight of the deep dark waters of the moat discourage you from the second option and you decide to crawl. Inching forward, you make your first foray . . . and find to your surprise that the surface of the bridge is less rough and sharp-edged than you had thought. By concentrating with all your will you can both keep your balance and avoid the roughest parts of the bridge. And you discover, to your amazement, that with each foot gained, you feel stronger, more filled with purpose. Slowly, the walls of the Grail Castle get nearer, until at last, to your great relief, you feel the soft earth beneath you. You fall face down on the greensward, almost hugging it with joy. . . Then, in a few minutes, when you are able to stand, you walk onward to the gates of the castle.

There, waiting to meet you, is a familiar figure. It is the Hermit whom you visited earlier. Smiling, he holds out his hands to you and welcomes you in. Few, he tells you, cross the Sword Bridge to this place, and those who do so are close to the Grail. It is not yet your time to look upon the vessel of healing – though that time will assuredly come – but he invites you to go with him and dine in the great hall, to sit where once Perceval sat, and to experience the subtle energies of the place. To this you agree and, though saddened that the Grail is not yet to be revealed, you accept that you have made an important step on your road to healing. You follow the Hermit into the great hall, where a sense of wonder almost overcomes you. So many have come here, and have experienced the power of the Grail. You sit at a plain wooden table and before you are set food and drink. You partake of these willingly, and realize as you do so that this is more than just sustenance for the tired body – it is food for the soul also, for this is a house where the soul feels especially cherished. As you sit in the Hall of the Grail, the wounds for which you have come to find healing are eased. You know that one day you will enter this place again, and that when you do the wonder you seek will be yours at last. . . Take a moment now to consider this truth in the depths of your spirit. . . [Pause].

In a while it is time to leave. You give thanks again to the Hermit, who blesses you and sends you upon your way with these words: 'Farewell, until we meet again. The King awaits you, his wounds cry out to be healed.'

Slowly, as you walk back through the great gates, the scene fades around you, and you are once again back where you began. But something has changed within you, you feel stronger and more able to face the perils which lie ahead on the road to the Wounded King.

Having looked at some of the underlying structures of the story of Perceval, it is time to begin our exploration of the second great story which deals with inner healing. In this we shall find ourselves led even deeper into the mystery at the heart of the Grail Quest, and take a step further on our own road to healing our wounded selves.

4 The Damsels of the Wells

Within this land is no tree leafy,
The meadows withered, the fountains dumb.
Yet from the mountains unto the valleys
A knight with piercing voice shall come.

Song of the Grail-less Lands Caitlín Matthews

THE STRICKEN LAND

In Chapters 2 and 3 we looked at the major texts which tell the story of the Wounded King and the Grail. There is one more important text, which will take us deeper still into the realm of the Grail, and show yet further aspects of the Wound and its potential for healing. To this end, the exercises in this chapter are all concerned with getting in touch with your inner self, and in imbibing the necessary wisdom and healing from those sources, which are uniquely able to offer the kind of healing you need at this point on the journey.

The name of the text is *The Elucidation*, and it was composed as a prequel to Chretien's poem, although it was written some time later (around 1225), and in fact has little or nothing to do with the earlier work. The story it tells is remarkable, and adds significantly to our understanding of the Wounded King. After a prologue in which we are told that the Grail is a secret which should not be spoken of openly, it begins by mentioning 'the rich country of Logres' (a name often applied to Arthur's Britain) 'whereof was much talk in days of yore'. Only one person can tell this story, and that is Master Blihis, who tells it now.

The kingdom turned to loss, the land was dead and desert in such wise as that it was scarce worth a couple of hazelnuts. For they lost the voices of the wells and the damsels that were therein. For no less thing was the service they rendered than this, that scarce any wandered by the way . . . but that . . . for drink and [food] he would go . . . far out of his way . . . to find one of the wells, and then nought could he ask for of fair [food] such as pleased him but . . . he should have it all so long as he asked in reason. For straightway . . . forth of the well issued a damsel – none fairer need he ask – bearing in her hand a cup of gold with larded meats, pasties and bread, while another damsel bore a white napkin and a dish of gold wherein was the [food] which he . . . had asked for. Right fair welcome found he at the well . . . The damsels with one accord served fair and joyously all wayfarers by the roads that came to the wells . . .(6)

Thus all is well in the land of Logres, but a threat looms large, in the form of a king who is another of what I have termed the 'Anti-Grail kings.' The story continues:

King Amangons, that was evil and craven-hearted, was the first to break the custom [of the Wells] for thereafter did many others the same according to the example they took from the king, whose duty it was to protect the damsels and to maintain and guard them with his peace. One of the damsels did he enforce, and to her sore sorrow did away her maiden head, and carried off from her the cup of gold . . . and afterwards did make him every day be served thereof . . . [And] thenceforth never did the damsel serve any more nor issue forth of that well for no man that might come thither to ask for victual. And all the other damsels only served in such sort as that none should see them. (ibid)

Following Amangons' example, his followers raped the damsels of the wells and carried off their golden cups. It is for this reason and no other, says the story-teller, that the land fell into ruin. For:

In such sort was the kingdom laid waste that thenceforth was no tree leafy. The meadows and the flowers were dried up and the waters were shrunken, nor [from thence onward] might no man find the Court of the Rich Fisherman that was wont to make in the land a glittering glory of gold and silver, of ermines and miner, or rich palls of sendell, of meats and of stuffs, of falcons gentle and merlins and tercels and sparrowhawks and falcons peregrine. (ibid)

THE WELLS OF LIFE

Here, then, is a very different account of the causes of the Waste
Land. In the beginning there are the Damsels of the Wells, who
are in some way connected to the Court of the Rich Fisher, but
who are under the protection of King Amangons. Their sole
task is to offer hospitality and food to weary travellers who, we
are told, go out of their way to experience this. Then Amangons,
having lusted after one of the damsels, casually rapes her and
steals her golden cup, which he then displays daily as a trophy
of his action. His followers follow suit until all the damsels are
raped and their golden cups stolen. This, we are told, is the
reason for the Waste Land, where 'no tree is leafy' and where
'the meadows and flowers are dried up'. Also, in some way, the
Court of the Rich Fisherman is no longer accessible, and with its
withdrawal go the richness and plenty which once marked out
the kingdom of Logres as the finest in the land. For, 'they lost
the voices of the wells and the damsels that were therein. . .'

So much in this is both new and fascinating that one scarcely
knows where to begin. Who, for instance, are the Damsels of
the Wells? If we are to understand the text correctly (and its
language is often obscure) they come 'out of' the wells when
called to by passing travellers. This suggests that they may well
be faery women, or even priestesses of some ancient sacred
well-cult, such as flourished for many hundreds of years in
Celtic Britain. An alternative reading in a German version of the
text reads damsels of the 'Mounds' rather than wells, which
again suggests a faery, or Otherworldly, connection.

Be that as it may, the important factors are that the maidens
are the guardians of certain sites (wells) which are almost
certainly sacred, that they possess golden cups and come forth
with offerings in a manner which sounds remarkably similar to
the Grail procession, and that they are in some way connected
to the Court of the Rich Fisherman, a shadowy alter-ego of the
Wounded King.

But with the actions of Amangons, who betrays his position
of trust and steals the virginity of the maidens as well as their
cups, there starts a period of deprivation where nothing grows
and where the richness which was freely available at the Court
of the Rich Fisherman is withdrawn. We may justly see the
Wells as a source of healing which becomes inaccessible after
the wounding of their guardians. Many of those who answered

the questionnaire saw the rape of the maidens as the rape of the inner self – in men as well as women – and expressed a desire to see justice done. Again, in more than half the responses I received, people expressed the feeling that even by simply reading the text they had taken the first step on the road to healing, though this was by no means easy for any of them.

Amangons is clearly another of the Anti-Grail kings typified by Clingsor and Garlon (their names are sufficiently similar to be identified as deriving from a common source). It is likely that Amangons is the Fisher King's brother, which would account for the dual links between both men and maidens. All of this is incredibly suggestive of a very different and possibly far older version of the Grail story.

The story now moves to Arthur's time, which by implication is some while later. When the Knights of the Round Table hear the story of the Damsels of the Wells they want to 'recover' them, and to 'destroy root and branch the kindred of them that had wrought them harm'. For it seems that Amangons' people have not ceased from the persecution of the damsels, but have actually taken to living near the Wells, so that if by chance any one of the women emerges, they are at once seized and killed.

Arthur's knights set forth in search of the Wells, but all those they discover are silent and deserted. Then, riding in the forest, they find a whole group of the maidens, accompanied by those knights who seek to protect them against attack. The Round Table knights join with these guardians and together they succeed in defeating the enemy. In the process Sir Gawain captures a knight named Blihos Bliheris (who may or may not be the same as the Blihis who is the supposed author of the text – the wording is unclear and the spelling slightly different) whom he sends back to Arthur in the customary fashion. But this man is more than a knight, he is also a story-teller, 'such as none could ever be weary of hearkening to his words', and soon has the entire court enthralled. Of course the most important story that everyone there wants to hear concerns the maidens and their companions encountered in the forest. Blihos responds willingly with another tantalizing fragment:

> Much marvel have ye of the damsels that ye see go among these great forests, and never make ye an end of asking in what country we are born. I will tell ye the truth thereof. We are all born of the damsels, who never in the world were fairer, whom King Amangons

did enforce. Never on any day of the world shall those wrongs be amended. The Peers of the Round Table of their courtesy and honour, of their prowess and valiance, are fain by force to recover the wells whereof these be the squires and knights and nobles. I will tell you the sum of the matter. These all [that is the Round Table Knights] shall journey in common, and the damsels likewise that wander through this country by forest and field . . . until such time as God shall give them to find the Court from whence shall come the joy whereby the land shall again be made bright. To them that shall seek the Court, shall befall adventures such as were never before found nor told of in this land before.(6)

Thus fired by the words of the story-teller, the knights go forth in search of the Rich Fisherman, who is curiously said to know 'much of nigromancy [magic], inasmuch that a hundred times changed he his semblance in such sort that those should have seen him in one guise should not know him again when he showed him as another man after another . . . fashion'. Gawain is said to have discovered the Court first, but it is Perceval who successfully asks the question regarding the Grail, though he forgets to ask concerning either the spear which bleeds or the broken sword. We are then treated to a description of the Grail King himself, and the way in which the sacred vessel comes and goes in that place. Again, there are significant variations from the versions we have been examining.

This is what Perceval sees;

By the space of three hours three times a day [were] their lamentations, so sore that no man, were he ever so hardy, but that if he should hear it he should be stricken with fear. Then did they hand four censers at four rich candlesticks that were at the horns of the bier. [On which, we were told previously, lay one who seemed dead.] When they had done the service, straightway the cries continued again, and every man vanished away. The hall that was great and wide remained void . . . and the stream of blood ran from the vessel where was the Lance through a rich channel of silver.

Then forthwith was the palace filled of the folk and the knights. Then was the fairest victual of the world made ready. Then issued forth in all his apparel the king that was unknown. From a chamber came he forth robed. In right noble attire he came, . . . and on his finger he had a ring exceeding good, and his arms he straightly folded, and upon his head a circle of gold whereof the stones are worth a treasure. Never so comely man on life could no man find. Right little might any surmise that this was he whom he [Perceval] had seen that day attired as a fisherman.

So soon as the king was seated, then might you see all the other knights seated at the other high tables. Then swiftly was the bread set on and the wine placed in presence in great cups of gold and silver. Thereafter you might see the Grail without servitor and without seneschal come through the door of a chamber and serve right worshipfully in rich dishes of gold that were worth a great treasure. The first meal did it set before the king, and then did it serve all the others round about, and nought less was it than a miracle . . . that it brought them . . . And then came the greatest miracle of all, whereunto is none other to be compared.(6)

At this point, infuriatingly, the poet declares that he cannot tell this part of story yet, as it does not belong here and all stories should be told in the right order. He then goes on to list a number of other episodes that he will tell in due course, including how 'the Good Knight shall come that found the Court three times, when shall you hear me recount point for point without feigning ought the truth as concerning the wells, whereunto they served, whereof these were the knights, and of the Grail wherefore it served, and all the manner of the Lance that bled . . .' Unfortunately, none of this has survived, if indeed it was ever written at all. The author goes on to say that the Court of the Rich Fisherman was found seven times, and that there are seven stories to tell concerning it, all of which he will relate in due course. He adds:

In very truth it was this finding of the Court and the Grail whereby the realm was repeopled, in such wise that the waters which ran not, and the fountains which flowed not, for that they had been dried up, ran forth [again] amidst the meadows. Then were the fields green and bountiful, and the woods clad in leaves the day that the Court was found. Throughout the country were the forests so thick, so fair and fresh, that every wayfarer journeying through the land did marvel thereat.

Finally we hear more of the history of the damsels. It appears that – either before or after the discovery of the Court, which is unclear – there came a folk who had themselves issued forth from the Wells, but who were of a very different sort to the damsels. They built castles and cities and strongholds for the maidens, including the famous Castle of Maidens, the Perilous Bridge and the Castle Orguellous (Castle of Pride). They then formed an Order of the Peers of the Rich Meinie in mocking echo of the Round Table fellowship, but filled with pride and

lack of pity. For four years Arthur makes war on them, until at last all call him master, and on that day is the Court of the Rich Fisherman (apparently) found. The poem ends on a curious note of disapproval 'that on the very day when the Court and the Rich Meinie were set free, they [that is the Knights of the Round Table] went a-hunting in the forest, and they that would fain go a-hawking followed the good rivers. This is how folk be of manner. Some will only have to do with disport, and others with how they shall apparel them. Nought did they but make merry the winter through until the summer.'

Thus ends this remarkable text, which is so different from, and yet which supplies a number of clues to, the story of the Grail and the Wounded King. I have given longer extracts here as the text is still generally unavailable (I hope to present a new translation and full commentary, much of it outside the scope of the present work, in the near future) and because of its importance to the argument presented here. For this is not simply another version of Chretien's text. It seems rather to preserve a genuinely ancient version of the Grail myth, in all probability dating from a time long before Christianity reached these lands, and it is important that it shifts the emphasis from the more masculine of the later Grail texts back to a deeper awareness of the importance of the divine feminine. This is itself inherent in the Grail story in virtually all its versions, but tends to be swamped by the theology and chivalry of the medieval epic tradition.

Unfortunately, much of *The Elucidation* is extremely opaque, and it trails off in an unsatisfactory and incomplete manner, promising to tell a whole string of further episodes which are then promptly forgotten. Despite this, we shall see as we examine it in more detail just how valuable it is as a document which adds significantly to our understanding both of the Grail myth and the story of the Wounded King in particular.

The Fountain, the Well and the Cauldron

The importance of the well as a symbol of life is well attested throughout the world, as is the idea that water contains the essence of life. This probably stems from the simple fact that we need water to sustain life, and that we emerged from the water and are made up of more than two-thirds of water ourselves.

But water is seen as a vehicle of life in a deeper sense, and this results in the idea of the Water of Life – to drink is to be restored – and to the many references to wells and fountains which contain an essence that is somehow more than just water.

The Celtic peoples in particular recognized this. Water was the way to the Otherworld, which was often represented as lying across the sea on an island; a vehicle for observing the mystery of being, and a substance which contained an element of fire – the fire of illumination which poets and other folk of skill sought above all else. Thus we have the early Irish story of Nechtan's Well, which contains not only water but also a brilliant light which can either blind those who look into it, or illuminate them with a powerful inspiration. This same idea is reflected in the concept of the *Imbas Forosna*, the 'Wisdom that illumines' which was understood as one of the prime initiatory secrets of the Celtic bards, as in the great Irish tale *Imacallam in da Thurad*, where it is said 'the poets thought that the brink of water was always a place of revelation and poetry'(40).

'We see by means of water,' says Wolfram von Eschenbach in Chapter 16 of *Parzival*(13). It is apparent within the stories that water is the bridge by which we cross the divide between ourselves and the Otherworldly realm of the Grail in which our soul-parts can be reunited. And it is by allowing the story of the Grail to work in us that our inner sight gains illumination, allowing us to perceive the vessel at last. We shall see how this is reflected in the stories when we come to explore the deeds of Gawain in the next chapter.

Images of wells, cauldrons and fountains as providers of wisdom and plenty occur in folk tradition all over the world. In the collection of the Grimm brothers there is a story called 'The Water of Life', in which a young man searches through the world for a healing draught to cure his sick father. With the help of a princess he finds his way to the fountain from which he must draw water before midnight. He succeeds, but as he departs the clock strikes twelve and the iron gate which protects the fountain slams shut, cutting off part of his heel. Like Perceval he is wounded in the attempt to bring healing to another; like Perceval, who is shut out of the Grail Castle by his inability to ask the question, the young man is shut out of the place where healing is available. In this we can see how similar the King and the Healer are: both are wounded, both find healing in the end, but only after a period of suffering and travail. Again, we learn that the healer, the wounded person and the healing are linked in a sequence which seldom varies throughout every version of the story.

Celtic tradition abounds in stories of cauldrons, wells and fountains. As we saw in Chapter 3 in the story of 'Branwen, Daughter of Llyr', a cauldron reanimates the dead warriors who are placed within it, and there is also the story of Taliesin, where the young proto-poet imbibes the three drops of wisdom from Ceridwen's cauldron. There are also the fountains such as the one at which Merlin finds healing for his madness, or where the waters of divine inspiration flow. The waters that arise in the Otherworld are almost always healing to mortals; they are charged with an energy which we lack, a completeness and connectedness which has the power to restore our wounded souls. Thus in the story of 'Cormac's Adventures in the Otherworld', we hear of the Fountain of Knowledge.

> . . . a shining fountain, with five streams flowing out of it, and the hosts in turn drinking the water. Nine hazels . . . grew over the well. The purple hazels dropped their nuts into the fountain and sent their husks floating down the streams. Now the sound of the falling of these streams was more melodious than any music that men sing.(1)

The five rivers flowing from this source are the senses; if they become dammed up, as when something happens to interrupt the flow of the healing waters, such as the rape of the maidens in The Elucidation, then we lose the ability to feel. And since we rely on our senses to interpret the world in which we live, we lose a vital part of our being. It is thus more than just the voices of the Wells that are taken from us when the inner Amangons attacks the inner maidens: we lose our ability to feel and to express those feelings as well. We are cut off from paradise, from knowledge and wisdom, from the knowledge of the senses, with a resultant woundedness and soul-loss.

At one level the urge which causes Amangons to attack the Maidens of the Wells is lust. At another it is a desire to possess the wisdom which is contained in the Wells which they guard. We can see this reflected in the Irish story, Feis Tighe Chonain(1), where the hero Fionn bathes in the magical lake of Slaib Cuilinn and loses his strength as a result. His followers, the Fian, lay siege to a nearby entrance to the Otherworld, until its lord, Cuilenn, comes forth and offers Fionn a draft from a golden cup which not only restores his vigour but also imparts wisdom to him.

This attack, like the assault upon the Wells, is fuelled by a desire for wisdom and power which are seen as deriving both from within the earth (the Wells) and the maidens who guard them. Both – maidens and earth – are feminine, so we are also witnessing a raid on the wisdom of the feminine, and in another sense an attempt to carry off the wisdom of the Otherworld, which is often freely given but which should never be forcefully taken. That the same thing happens within ourselves is all too obvious. On the surface we denigrate the earth and the feminine principle; inwardly we long for it. When the feminine strain in men is ignored, the masculine part overwhelms and invades the feminine and the result is the beginning of an inner Waste Land. Nor is this by any means limited to men. Women also can, and do, deny their feminine side, resulting in an imbalance which is just as potentially wounding.

Once again the Grail has a lesson for us; the story of the Maidens of the Wells shows what can occur when the feminine is defiled, while in the story as told by Chretien the balancing of the Grail's feminine wisdom with that of the masculine spear are shown to be polarized in the wounding/healing of the individual.

The myth of the Waste Land is about separation, division, the loss of the feminine and the neglect of our emotional life. The waters of life well up from the fountain, the well and the cauldron; when we lose the Voices of the Wells, and their restoring waters, we lose our connection to life itself; our grasp of the essential nature of humanity is loosened and we slip away into a place where meaning almost ceases. Yet the healing of the land and the Quest for the Grail is about restoring, among other things, the polarity between the masculine and the feminine. It is not accidental that the story often ends in marriage – of Perceval to Blanchflor, man to woman, masculine to feminine.

It is this which makes the loss of the Wells so shocking, for when Amangons acts, the benefits which derive from them are dammed up. The land becomes barren and suffering is everywhere. The Damsels of the Wells depart, taking the wisdom of the Wells with them. They take the reproductive function with them; as with the Wounded King, there can be no further generation within the Waste Land while they are absent. And yet, they continue. Do they reproduce with each other – are they gathered together in one place or group, bound by their common suffering and grievance? Here we enter a larger picture, one which deals with cultural separation and collective suffering. It is the curse of the maidens that they must bear the children of their ravishers, and it is the curse of those children to be the product of mixed marriages. These kinds of wounds are apparent everywhere today – in Bosnia, in former Yugoslavia, and in Ireland – where cultural differences and blood feuds continue to tear apart the land and the people.

The Grail stories reflect this in the whole idea of dislocation and barrenness which is at the heart of the Wounded King's land. It shows up in the repeated references to vengeance and betrayal which appear in many of the stories from *Peredur*(10) to *Le Morte Darthur*(12). The rottenness at the heart of the kingdom, personified by Garlon, by Amangons, and by Clingsor, goes unchecked until the actions of an outsider, Perceval or Balin, bring about a recognition of the darkness which can subsequently be integrated into the healed body of the king and the land. These wounds are as difficult to write about as they are to deal with, and they fall to some extent outside the range of this book. Nonetheless we should recognize that it is by healing the wounds within ourselves that we can bring about healing on a global scale.

Exercise 8 The Waters of Life

We need the Waters of Life in order to live fully and creatively; their lack is one of the primary ways in which our wounds are sustained. To suffer the Waste Land experience within ourselves is to feel 'dried up' in every sense of the word. To bring ourselves back to an awareness of our fruitful selves we need to visit the Otherworld and drink deeply. In the exercise which follows, which is a visualization, we shall do just that.

Close your eyes and allow your consciousness to move from everyday reality to subtle reality, where a scene opens before you . . .

You are standing before the entrance to a low cave-mouth, set in the side of a low rounded hill. You become aware that a most wonderful scent is issuing forth from within it, compounded of all the most wonderful things you have ever smelled – the very essence of smell! Drawn thither by a desire to discover more, you enter the cave and find yourself following a narrow passageway that leads deep into the earth . . .

In a matter of moments you emerge from the other end of the passage, and find that you are inside a cavern of such vast proportions that you cannot see the far walls, and are only dimly aware of the roof, far above you. Although you are far beneath the earth this is no dark or gloomy place, but a land full of light, which issues from no visible source, but which is as bright as the sun at noon. There is grass here, growing soft beneath your feet, and a road leads away into the distance, bordered by trees and hedgerows full of bright unfamiliar flowers. You begin to follow the path, and soon notice a curious thing – though you seem to be walking at a normal pace, the distance you have covered is vastly greater than that in the ordinary world. As you look back, the wall of the cavern, and the entrance by which you came in, are already far distant . . .

Looking ahead again you see, neither near nor far, a low cluster of bui'dings. Even as you see them you are somehow brought closer, and in a moment you are standing before a long, low-lying wooden house, with a high peaked roof thatched with what at first seems like a straw but which, as you look more closely, seems as though it were pure gold . . .

Tall pillars flank the open doorway, intricately carved with spirals, from the depth of which look out curious, ancient faces, the eyes of which seem to follow you as you enter . . . Inside all is cool and dim, and it takes a moment for your eyes to adjust. Then you see before you a long hall, with tall tree-like columns supporting the roof, and a floor of beaten earth. At the far end is a raised platform, on which is a tall, high-backed chair, occupied by a seated figure. You hesitate for a moment until beckoned forward to stand before the chair . . .

Looking up, you see that the figure is heavily veiled in such a manner that you cannot say whether it is man or woman, old or young. Then you hear a voice, which communicates itself to you in such a way that you do not actually hear it with your ears, but with your whole being. At this level it has no gender, but is interpreted by you according to your needs . . .

'Why have you come?' demands the voice, neither kindly nor sternly.

'To drink of the Water of Life,' you hear yourself answering.

'Many seek to do this, but few understand what it means,' answers the voice within you.

'I seek enlightenment and healing,' you reply.

For a time there is no answer, and yet you feel that you are being scrutinized deeply, to the very core of your being. This may seem uncomfortable, but try to be open and at peace as far as you are able . . .

After a short space of time the figure moves almost imperceptibly, and you see that a great golden cup is revealed, standing on a pillar by the side of the chair. Then you hear the voice again within you. It may invite you to drink, or it may tell you that the moment is not yet come when it is appropriate for you to do so. If the former, you should go forward and raise the cup to your lips. If the latter, give thanks to the veiled one and take your leave, returning by way of the hall, the bright landscape and the passage between the worlds. If you are permitted to drink, do so and remain in silence for a time as you experience the effects of the Water of Life upon you . . . [Pause].

Whatever the outcome, when you are ready, give thanks to the figure on the chair and depart from the hall. Outside, the path through the bright land stretches before you. Follow it and in no time at all you will find yourself back at the entrance to the passageway by which you entered this place. Go through it and emerge into the outside world. Take your time to re-establish normal consciousness and write down everything you felt and experienced in the Otherworld.

The Voices of the Wells

A number of those who answered the questionnaire noted that in the Maidens of the Wells story, the phrase 'they lost the voices of the wells' reminded them of their own personal loss of voice (of self and identity), wounds inflicted upon them by society. One wrote 'I'm aware of how programmed I am to be a victim', a factor that we tend to ignore when it surfaces in our own lives, but which we can see clearly enough in others. And as the gifted healer Carolyn Myss remarks 'Victims cannot heal'(46). This comes out of an addiction to the power of the wound, in which we become all too willing to harvest the pain, fear and glamour of our wounds, rather than giving them up or actively seeking healing.

Some of this is habitual: we are used to feeling the way we do, and find it increasingly hard to shift into another mode of thought. Our minds like to take certain pathways. Just as we follow a physical route which we know gets us to our destination in the least possible time, or which takes us through the most beautiful countryside, so our minds will follow a route we have laid down for them. If this is an aimless, wandering path, like that followed by Perceval during his five years in the wilderness, than we too will lose ourselves. If the path leads back to some moment of past pain – such as the memory of Perceval's mother which is always flashing through his mind – then the mind will dwell in that wound. It will even feed off that wound, increasing its energy, while the rest of the wounded person shrivels up inside. The result is an ever-deepening wound over which we have less and less control.

The best way to combat this is to acknowledge the existence of the wound, and then to take away its power. If we give it more and more power – like the man I knew who used to introduce himself with the words 'Hello, I'm Bill – I'm divorced' – it will eventually overwhelm us. If, on the other hand, we made a determined call to our inner helpers to help us recognize the wound for what it is and to work towards its healing, then we have taken a hugely important step.

Exercise 9 The Voices of the Wells

Not only do we see by means of water, we also hear. The Voices of the Wells speak clearly within us if we let them, and by listening we hear what we need to know about our own healing. In this next exercise you will make a shamanic journey to the Underworld to find the Maidens of the Wells and ask them for the wisdom they hold to be released within you. You may, if you desire, ask concerning any one of your own wounds, or for the healing of any aspect of your inner self that you recognize as needing it. Or, if you have experienced difficulty in acknowledging the wounds you carry, you may ask for help with this. As always follow the instructions on pp. 13–16, and take the Questing Beast with you as guide and counsellor. Ask to be taken to one or more of the maidens, and remember to be as clear as you can, before you begin, about which of your wounds you are seeking help. The maiden may not give you direct healing – though this is by no means impossible – but she will offer advice or instruction in ways that you can work on yourself. Be sure to remember this if you are not journeying aloud, and write down everything you can recall when the journey is ended.

THE SOUL OF THE LAND

At a deep level the story of the Maidens of the Wells is about the loss of a personal relationship between ourselves and the land on which we live. We need to preserve this if we are to maintain our soul-health, which suffers when we are dislocated from the earth. When the land is sick we are sick, and vice versa; we draw our nourishment from the earth in much the same way that a plant does, except that our roots are invisible. They are no less important for that, and if we ignore them, or cut them off, the flow of nutrients ceases.

All of the myths of the wounded land concern this. As already noted, in the Arthurian mythos there is a certain sense in which the Wounded King is a surrogate for Arthur: he suffers for the actual monarch, who may at one time have been identified with the actual Wounded King. This is implicit in most of the versions, and is the probable reason why Arthur himself does not go on the Quest for the Grail, but sends his fellowship of knights in his stead. And if the Wounded King is Arthur's surrogate, might he not be, figuratively speaking, Arthur's lost soul? This is by no means unlikely; one has only to think of the many folk stories from around the world in which a protagonist – usually a giant – has the ability to remove his heart and hide it somewhere, so that the hero has to find the heart in order to kill him. If the heart can be removed and hidden, why not the soul? Certainly, in cases of soul-loss there are plenty of examples of people who have voluntarily given up their soul-parts, and hidden them, and where the shaman has to hunt to find them.

It seems to me that this is what the Quest Knights are doing for Arthur. By seeking the Grail (which is itself both a symbol of the heart and the soul) and in their desire to heal the Wounded King, they are in fact seeking to heal Arthur, and through him the Waste Land, which is by extension the whole of Britain rather than simply the country around the Grail Castle. And if Arthur's soul is truly lost, then the need of the land is indeed that it should be restored, just as, when our own soul-parts go missing, we need to retrieve them for ourselves, or visit a shaman to have them retrieved for us.

All this ties in with the age-old idea of the relationship of king to land, a concept understood by the Celtic peoples in particular, and by many other cultures in the ancient world. For them, the person of the king was sacrosanct; he had to be in perfect health, and perfect physically, in order to reign. Thus for example in the Irish myth of Nuadh the hero was forced to give up his place to another when he lost a hand in battle.

But the concept had a deeper concomitant. In Irish tradition the king married the land in a ritual called *banai righi*, the Wedding Feast of Kingship, which often included an actual bonding between the king and a woman who represented the Sovereignty of the land. Numerous mythic stories exist which describe the testing of the future monarch by the Goddess of the Land, and these are similar to the encounters between the Quest Knights and the Hideous Damsel, of whom we shall learn more in the next chapter.

All these stories demonstrate clearly that the king had to be perfect because of this relationship. If he was somehow imperfect, the land was also: the relationship between man and goddess became damaged. It is to this idea that we can trace the close links between the Wounded King and the Waste Land; neither can be restored until the other is healed.

This idea is expressed repeatedly in Celtic myth and literature. Thus in the story of the Cairbre Cinnchait, who won the kingdom of Ireland by violence and mercilessly killed all the children of the nobles to ensure his status, all the corn in the land bore but a single ear, and every oak produced only a single acorn. Once the deposed dynasty returned to the throne, however, the land recovered its fertility. As late as the 12th century, at the time when the Grail works were being composed, we find a poem which has the line 'We shall have bad years and long days with false kings and failed crops.'(8)

The king's relationship to the land is very like the relationship between body and soul. When the soul is sick the body becomes sick; when the king is sick the land is sick also. Thus when we work upon the subtle relationship between body and soul, we are in fact carrying out a parallel work of healing to that undertaken by Perceval and his like in healing the Wounded King.

One of the names by which Perceval is known is 'He Who Frees the Waters'. This refers to the fact that, when the Grail question is asked, water flows again in the dead land, bringing fruition to the plants and creatures who live there. It can also mean one who frees the waters of the spirit, or of the emotions. When old, dammed-up feelings are released, healing nearly always follows, whether it comes from the release of long rankling anger, or the considered examination of an old wound that has never fully healed. In the context of the stories we have been exploring, in particular that of the Maidens of the Wells, this freeing of the waters means that the land is once again made fruitful; in the context of our own search for healing, it means that we are in touch with our emotional selves, with the water of life, and are once again rooted in the land.

Nor is it without significance that the Wounded King is also called the Fisher King or the Rich Fisherman. In effect he is casting his line into the waters of the soul to bring forth a healer; he can still practise a degree of autonomy which will ultimately help him towards a whole state. In the same way, we can help ourselves, encouraging the dammed-up waters to flow again in our hearts and minds, calling out to the hero within to take on the role of healer.

In terms of our own experience we may choose to view the Wounded King in a number of ways: as a representative of ourselves, or of the wounded people who seek healing but cannot find it without the help of a specific healer, or as an image of the part of our soul which relates to the land on which we live and have our being, and which is far more than the lifeless chunk of rock that we have tended to see in the last few centuries. Discovering a more spiritual connection with the earth is an important step on the road to healing. Until we are able to perceive the earth as a living being with which we have a close and personal relationship, we will find it that much harder to see the nature of our own wounds and address their healing.

This should not be a difficult thing to do. Respect for the land is already deeply seeded within us. Why else do we get angry when a new road is driven through a place of natural beauty, or when a site that has never known habitation is suddenly turned into a housing estate? This deep love of the land is what makes us tie ourselves to trees about to be felled, or lie down in the road in front of bulldozers about to plough through the heritage of fields and meadows. If we truly feel this, then we already possess the energy to begin healing the divide between ourselves and the land, and between ourselves and the rest of the cosmos.

Exercise 10 The Sacred Earth

This exercise is designed to help us recognize the powerful inner dimension of the earth. Curiously enough it involves us in a shamanic journey which takes place indoors and away from the outer source of such an awareness. In my own practice I seldom ask my students to journey at a sacred site, a situation which frequently causes puzzlement. The truth of the matter is that the shaman accesses a different level of reality, and that therefore to visit an actual site from this other perspective opens the way to an experience of the real place. Hence the shaman will generally visit a sacred site first, then journey back to it in subtle reality.

For the purposes of this exercise, you should prepare for a Middleworld Journey, a journey which leads into the subtle echo of this world. Follow the instructions on pp xxi–xxii and 13–16. You should be lying down, relaxed and comfortable, with a drumming tape ready to play. The journey is to a place in nature which you know well. It can be a park or garden if you live in a city, otherwise any place in the land to which you are accustomed to visit and where you feel comfortable. Remember that all the land is sacred, so it does not necessarily have to be a sacred site such as a stone circle or Neolithic grave-mound. The object of the journey is to visit this place and to ask your guide or helper (whether it is the Questing Beast or some other with whom you are used to working) to show you its true quality. The very fact of journeying there at all will open this level of awareness within you; but here you are seeking a deeper experience which will make you more aware of the connection between yourself and the earth. Take time to accustom yourself to this very different level of awareness, and be aware of as much as you can. On returning, note down as many details of the experience as you can – though the chances are that it will be such a powerful experience that you will not easily forget it.

THE WOUNDED MAIDEN

We have seen how many of the wounds we experience derive from a spiritual source, and how the same is true of the healing process, which works at a soul-level within us. The subtlety of the process, which is often incremental, revealed in small shifts of consciousness and awareness, is all a part of this. One such shift is that from victim to healer, and this change is perfectly exemplified in the character and story of one of the least-known figures in the Grail myth: Dindraine, the sister of Perceval, who may be seen as a Wounded Maiden.

Brought up in isolation, like her brother, she elects to follow the path of solitary devotion to God: she becomes an anchoress, living alone in a cell in the woods. It is there that she receives a vision of the Grail, significantly before it appears at Camelot, and when the great Quest begins she accompanies the three most successful knights, including her brother, on their journey. Arriving at a castle where a woman lies sick with leprosy, she learns that the custom of the place requires that any virgin who comes that way give some of her blood to heal the wounded woman. Her knightly companions would have defended her against this practice, but Dindraine announces that she will freely give her blood. A vein in her arm is opened, but too much blood is taken and she begins to die. Welcoming death, she instructs her companions to place her body in the magical ship which has carried them thither, and to set it adrift on the open sea. They do so and when, later on, they arrive at the sacred city of Sarras where the Grail is to be housed, they find that her uncorrupted remains have arrived before them. After the final miracles of the Grail she is buried alongside her spiritual brother Galahad (who in this version of the story supersedes Perceval as the Grail winner).

Dindraine is thus the first to see the Grail and the first to arrive at the celestial city where it is to be housed. She is a way-shower who goes before all in the spirit. Her voluntary sacrifice makes her a healer in the tradition of the Grail, and it is not without significance that she heals through the giving of blood, let out of her arm in a marvellous echo of the Grail King's wound. But, unlike the Wounded King (whose niece or even daughter she may well be if one accepts alternative traditions), the letting of her blood acts as a healing medium, rather than a curse which inflicts sterility on the land.

In many ways Dindraine is synonymous with the Sorrowful Maiden of the Waste Land, who is often mourning the death of her lover. But the true nature of Dindraine is to transform sorrow into joy, to transcend the negative moment when all seems dark and terrible. She experiences all that life can offer even before leaving her hermit's cell, and when the terrors and dangers of the world threaten to overwhelm her, she changes her life, transmuting death itself into the life of the spirit.

In another sense she fulfils the role of Sovereignty, dispensing the bounty of healing through the pouring out of her life blood. In the Irish tale of *Baile in Scail* (The Phantom's Prophecy) Sovereignty pours out different liquids from different cups. In the story the hero Conn encounters her seated in a chair surrounded by different containers. She asks the god Lugh for whom she should pour and is told it is Conn, thus indicating that he will be king(4). According to one of the oldest traditions of Sovereignty she proffers three drinks: the Red Drink of Lordship (kingship), the white milk of fostering (strength), and the dark drink of forgetting (healing). Dindraine, in pouring forth her blood, is offering a healing draught. She gives of her blood in the same unstinting way as the pelican which, in medieval times, was believed to tear its breast in order to feed its young with its own blood. The Well Maidens are indeed her spiritual daughters, giving the bounty of their compassionate wisdom to all.

In a telling episode from the 13th-century romance of *Perlesvaus*(15), Dindraine undergoes the adventure of the Perilous Cemetery, a haunted place to which few of the knights dare go, and from which those who do seldom return. There, in order to

obtain a piece of the relic of Christ's shroud she must face
ghostly knights armed with flaming spears. Dindraine attains
the cemetery, seizes hold of the shroud and is at once told
(falsely as it transpires) by a disembodied voice that the Fisher
King is dead, the Grail withdrawn from human sight or attain-
ment, and the King of Castle Mortal (another of the Anti-Grail
kings) has triumphed. Dindraine is almost despairing at this,
but her courage is such that she refuses to give up, and with the
help of her brother achieves her desired goals. Dindraine's own
words to Perceval as she sets out for the cemetery are telling
indeed: 'Look at *my* path, it is little frequented, for I tell you, no
knight dares take it without grave peril to himself and deep
fear: may God guard your body, for mine will be in great danger
tonight.' She goes armed, not with the armour of chivalry, but
with the courage of her spiritual determination.

Dindraine's selfless courage in giving up her blood (changing
her life) contributes to the healing of the Wounded King as well
as to her own future. She is able to understand and interpret
the Dolorous Blow, the Wound, because she undergoes it, in
actuality as a woman, and symbolically in her physical wounding. Her wound is in the arm rather than the thigh, and it is
possible to see this as a wounding in the creative activity,
expressed through the arm and hand, so that there is a parallel
between Dindraine's wounding and the damaged generative
aspect of the Grail King.

But Dindraine transcends this with her courage and vision.
We, in our own quest for healing and restitution, inevitably
encounter the dark places of our soul, our own perilous chapels,
where we will be asked to give up a great deal. This symbolic
blood-letting, however, leads not to an actual death, but to what
we might think of as a 'change of blood', a re-awakening to the
bountiful energies of the inner life – healing for the parched
earth and the parched soul.

In this way Dindraine's role comes into focus as a healer
of ancestral wounds. The woman who is healed suffers from a
disease of the blood, which is the carrier of more than genetic
memory. Many of our wounds are inherited, ancestral problems
passed on down the blood line. The old blood of the sick
woman is tainted; Dindraine replaces it with her own. She
frees the waters of the blood as Perceval frees the waters of the
soul.

Healing follows the spiritual discovery of the causes of

woundedness. Perceval has to journey on a long and difficult Quest to find his way back to the mysteries of the heart from which he was never far at any time, though he failed to realize this. Dindraine was always in touch, knew of the coming of the Grail before any of the Quest knights, and, in the end, she crosses the divide between life and death, between the outer and inner worlds, before any of those who set forth from Camelot. In this way she is a way-shower, and it is important that we recognize her as a type of wounded healer rather than as a victim. Her blood becomes a bridge between the worlds, as well as a means of healing the leprous woman. Her giving of blood is an image that reconnects us, re-establishes the ways between the worlds.

Exercise 11 The Perilous Chapel

Facing the perils of life is never easy, yet we do so in one way or another, on an almost daily basis. The difference between the passive acceptance of these troughs, and an active transmutation of them into positive and healing experiences, is only a small step. Not always an easy step, but still a small one. It is indeed rather like the step from outer reality to inner, from the normal world to the Otherworld. In this next exercise you will be called upon to face one of your deepest fears, and helped to transform it into something other. To do this you will be helped by Dindraine, who as we have seen represents the ability to transform the nature of woundedness into a healing experience. This is indeed one of the most profound mysteries of the Grail myth – the opportunity which is offered to those who seek it, to transmute one kind of experience into another, to replace suffering with joy, negative with positive, to re-establish the fruitful earth where once the Waste Land held sway.

Prepare yourself for a visualization, closing your eyes and allowing your surroundings to fade into the background . . . as the shift in consciousness takes place you find yourself once again in a forest of mighty trees. Ahead of you lies a path, leading deeper into the tangled heart of the forest. You follow it cautiously, aware that there may be dangers ahead, for this is a place seldom visited by anyone, for all that the path seems broad and well-trodden . . .

Ahead now you see a clearing amid the trees, a place that must once have been less overgrown, but which is now almost covered by undergrowth which has overtaken the place. You see where a small, low-roofed building stands, surrounded by an ancient cemetery. The remains of old broken crosses and headstones rear up from the tangled nettles and spiralling brambles, their inscriptions barely readable. The remains of shattered glass in the windows and the shape of a stone cross carved above the leaning door tell you that the building was once a chapel. Now it has a deserted and somewhat sinister look which makes you reluctant to approach. But you remind yourself that you came here to discover healing and truth, and so you go forward . . .

Almost at once you feel a wave of fear. Shapes seem to move at the edge of your sight, though never completely visible. You hesitate, feet dragging in the tangled grass and weeds which spring up on every side. And as you pause a figure emerges from the broken doorway of the chapel – a dark indistinct shape whose eyes gleam redly, and who carries a spear which seems to burn from haft to tip, yet is never consumed. The fire is a cold fire, and it turns your heart to ice . . .

Though the figure speaks no words, you hear a voice in your head, demanding to know why you have come there. Now is the time you must summon up all your courage and state the reason why you have come, naming some wound or wounds that you carry, and giving them form if need be . . .

In answer the figure laughs mockingly, questioning not only your right to be there, but your ability to face up to as much as a single note of pain or suffering . . .

There is only one way that you can answer. Pull out from deep within yourself an image of your greatest fear, your worst nightmare, and look at it directly as you would at an adversary who threatened your very life . . . [Pause]

As you struggle with the pain and fear that has grown fat within you, you become aware of a second figure, who has appeared from amid the trees. It is a woman, clad in white, who seems to gleam out like a light amid the darkness of that place. As she comes to stand beside you, you feel enveloped in the warmth of her presence, and suddenly neither your pain nor the dark figure before you seem so absolute. Drawing upon the strength of the woman at your side you face your deepest enemy . . . [Pause]

At last you have done all that you can, and as you become fully aware of the clearing again you see that the dark and mocking figure has vanished, and with it much of the gloom and fearfulness of that place. The woman alone stands before you now, and in her hands is a golden cup filled to the brim with clear liquid. You look into her face for the first time, and see a lovely and peaceful visage, lit by bright and dancing eyes. She smiles and holds out the cup to you. 'I am Dindraine,' she says. 'Drink of the Cup of Replenishment and Love.' You take the proffered vessel and drink deeply of the liquid, which seems to you like nothing so much as pure light . . . As you do so, be aware that you are imbibing strength and vitality, and something more – food for the soul, and healing for the deepest wounds . . .

When you have drunk, you return the cup to Dindraine, who now invites you to walk with her for a time, and to speak about any of the wounds you have borne or which you still bear. Take your time to do this, for you will hear only wisdom from the lips of Perceval's sister . . . [Pause]

When you are ready, prepare to take your leave of Dindraine, thanking her for the help she has given you. She tells you that you may return again at any time, and that for you this place will hold no terrors henceforward. Slowly the scene fades from your consciousness and you reawaken, refreshed, to the outer world.

You have now completed another important stage on the road to healing. In the next chapter we turn towards powerful inner sources which enable us enter even more deeply into the mythology of woundedness, and which offer still further means to activate the healing energies already present within us.

5   The Loathly Bride

And as he rode upon a moor
He saw a lady where she sat
Betwixt an oak and a green hollen –
She was clad in red scarlet.

The Wedding of Sir Gawain Anon

THE LOATHLY LADY

The encounter with the Loathly Lady or Hideous Damsel is one of the most important tests to be encountered by the Quest knights, and it is much the same for ourselves. She is there to tell us why and how we are wounded, if we are not sufficiently in touch to know for ourselves, and to offer ways that we may seek healing. Her hideous nature is an expression of the woundedness of women (as in the raped Damsels of the Wells), just as the dry land is symptomatic of the neglect and fear of the feminine which is one of its primary causes. Yet the Loathly Lady has another side – she is the wisdom of the feminine, the teacher and helper who may use rough words to spur us on, but without whose help we may never reach our goal.

It is after his first visit to the Grail Castle, where he has failed to ask the question, that Perceval meets the Loathly Lady for the first time. In Chretien's poem she is nameless, in Wolfram's *Parzival* (13) she is called Cundry; her description in both works is powerful and graphic:

Her hair hung in two tresses, black and twisted; and if the words of my source are true, there was no creature so utterly ugly even in Hell. You have never seen iron as black as her neck and her eyes were just two holes, tiny as the eyes of a rat; her nose was like a cat's or a monkey's, her lips like an ass's or a cow's; her teeth were so discoloured that they looked like egg-yolk; and she had a beard like a Billy-goat. She had a hump in the middle of her chest and her back was like a crook. Her loins and shoulders were perfect for leading a dance, for she had a curve in her back and haunches that bent like willow-wands.(14)

This terrifying figure proceeds to castigate Perceval for not asking the question, and tells him of all the sorrows that will come about as a result. In Chretien's version of the story she is described in terms which make much use of animal imagery. In the 14th-century poem *The Wedding of Sir Gawain and Dame Ragnell* (17), at which we shall look more closely later, she has boar's tusks, pig's bristles, a doglike nose, bear's ears, and claws like a lion. This imagery is not without its significance. It is reminiscent of the shamans who partake of animals' powers and occasionally take on the actual shape of their animal helpers. Cundry derives a great deal of her power from the natural world; indeed, she may be said to represent nature. In the myth her role is that of a messenger to those who seek the healing of the king and the land; to those of us who seek healing for ourselves, she performs the same function. She is the voice that speaks in our own hearts, warning us that the wounds we possess are growing deeper or wider, and that if we do not take action it may be too late. She is the challenger who forces us to come to terms with our woundedness and take action to find healing. She exists to make us question our most deeply held preconceptions; by interacting with her we are exploring some of the deepest and most primal causes of the wound.

In a medieval Irish tale, 'The Adventures of the Sons of Eochaid Mugmedon', we meet her under her proper title of 'Sovereignty'. In this story we hear of the seven sons of Ireland's king, one of whom is to be chosen as his successor. Various tests are prepared for the boys, the last of which is to send them out hunting. Together they capture and kill a boar, light a fire and prepare to spend the night outdoors. But they are soon thirsty, and one by one go out in search of water. One by one they return, empty-handed, having encountered a fearsome hag guarding the only well in close proximity. From each boy she demands a kiss in return for a drink, and all refuse her except for the youngest, Niall. He is the last to go to the well-side and this is what he sees:

... every joint and limb of her, from the top of her head to the earth, was as black as coal. Like the tail of a wild horse was the grey bristly mane that came through the upper part of her head-crown. The green branch of an

oak in bearing would be severed by the sickle of green teeth that lay in
her head and reached to her ears. She had a middle fibrous, spotted with
pustules, diseased, and shins distorted and awry. Her ankles were thick,
her shoulders were broad, her knees were big, and her nails were green.(20)

Again we see the imagery of an animal and of the living earth.
Niall agrees not only to kiss her but to lie with her as well.
When he touches her lips she is transformed.

> *. . . there was not in the world a damsel whose gait nor appearance were*
> *more lovable than hers! . . . Plump and queenly forearms she had; fingers*
> *long and lengthy; calves straight and beautifully coloured. Two blunt*
> *shoes of white bronze between her little, soft-white feet and the ground. A*
> *costly full-purple mantle she wore, with a brooch of bright silver in the*
> *clothing of her mantle. Shining pearl teeth she had, an eye large [and]*
> *queenly, and lips red as rowanberries. (ibid)*

As soon as Niall goes beyond the outer form towards the inner
beauty of the hag, she is transformed. This is the very heart of
the myth of Sovereignty, and it concerns not only the way in
which we, as ordinary people, relate to the land, but also the
way in which we relate to our wounds. If we perceive them
only as horrible, fearsome things, which must be overcome
rather than accepted, then of course we shall see them in
the form of the Hideous Damsel or the Loathly Lady. If, on the
other hand, we can see the positive aspects of woundedness,
then we shall have made an important move towards healing.
In the same text quoted above, Sovereignty later says of herself:

> *And as you saw me loathsome, bestial, and horrible at first, but at last*
> *beautiful, even so is royal rule. The land cannot be won without battles*
> *and conflicts, but in the end everyone finds that sovereignty is both*
> *beautiful and glorious.(30)*

This is a wonderfully clear statement; the Loathly Lady may
appear hideous, just as the trials and tribulations of life can
loom large and at times ugly; but once we have faced up to the
'battles and conflicts', in the end 'to everyone [she] is good and
beautiful'.

FACING THE HAG

However, the character is much more than this, and to discover
what we need to look at one more story. Although on the face

of it this is not a Grail text, it does have much to tell us about the wounds that manifest in women, and the nature of the Loathly Lady. Indeed, this text can be said to 'complete' the story of the Hideous Damsel, as she appears in Chretien and Wolfram and nearly all the other Grail texts.

The story is told in a medieval poem called *The Wedding of Sir Gawain and Dame Ragnell* (17). It exists in several versions between the 14th and 15th centuries, the fullest and most satisfactory of which is contained in a unique manuscript preserved in the Bodleian Library, Oxford. The story it tells is this:

The story of Gawain and Ragnell

One day King Arthur went hunting in the woods. He sighted a great and beautiful hart and pursued it alone. He killed the deer and was about to skin it when an extraordinary figure appeared, tall and powerful and clad in full armour. He threatened the king and demanded reparation for the awarding of his lands to Sir Gawain, who was the king's nephew. Arthur asked his name and was told that it was Sir Gromer Somer Jour. Since the king was unarmed save for a hunting bow and spear he was at a disadvantage. Gromer courteously allowed him a chance to save his life. One year hence he must return, alone, to that same place with the answer to a question: 'What is it women most desire?' To this Arthur gave his promise, and returned home full of sadness, for he thought that he would never find the answer. Sir Gawain soon noticed that something was wrong, and when pressed the king poured out the story of his meeting with Gromer. Gawain told him to be of good cheer, for they would set out together and ride to distant lands, asking every woman they met for the answer and writing them all down in a great book. The king thought this a fine idea, and they set forth at once, each one taking a different road to increase the area they covered.

Along the road they met many women, and every one they asked the question. Some said they liked to be finely dressed, others that they liked to be flattered, still others spoke of a lusty man in their arms. Both Gawain and the king wrote everything down, and when they returned to the court a year later they each had a huge collection of answers.

Accordingly, on the day appointed, King Arthur set out for the forest. Along the way he met with a woman carrying a lute on her back. She was the most hideous creature the king had ever seen. Her face was red, her nose snotty, her mouth wide, her teeth yellow, her eye rheumy. Her teeth stuck out from between her lips, and her cheeks were as fat as a normal woman's hips. Her shoulders were broad, her neck long and her hair clotted. Her breasts were huge. Nothing could adequately describe her hideousness, and yet she rode upon a fine horse, with a decorated bridle, and her manner was polite. She greeted Arthur and told him that she was aware of the reason for his journey, and that it would fail unless she told him the one right answer. In return for this, she required only one thing – the person of Sir Gawain in marriage!

Horrified, the king insisted that he could not speak for his nephew, but that he would do all that he could to bring about her wish. With this she declared herself satisfied, and told him that her name was Ragnell. The king returned to the court and the first person he met was Gawain, who asked him how he had fared. Arthur told him of his meeting with Ragnell and of the sorrow he felt because of it. Gawain at once replied cheerfully that he would willingly marry the woman, though she was as ugly as sin, if it would save the king's life. Arthur swore that Gawain was the best knight he had ever known, and set out again for the forest. He soon met Ragnell, who was waiting for him, and relayed to her the news that Gawain was willing to marry her. She clapped her hands and told him the answer to Gromer's riddle, warning the king that he would be angry, but that he would have no power over him.

Arthur rode on his way until he met with Gromer, to whom he gave the two books of answers which Gawain and he had gathered. Gromer looked at each of them, then threw them aside and drew his sword. 'Wait,' said King Arthur, 'I have one more answer yet.' And he told Gromer what Ragnell had said. As she had predicted, the answer made Gromer furious. 'Only one woman could have told you that,' he cried, 'and that is my sister Dame Ragnell.' He cursed her roundly, but agreed that the king had won. Arthur rode home in a good mood, until he met the hideous Ragnell on the road. She reminded him of his promise, and Arthur reluctantly agreed that she had saved him. He set off for the court with Ragnell riding a little way behind him. They entered the court together and Ragnell ordered the king to send for Sir Gawain, so that she might hear it from his own lips that he was ready and willing to marry her.

There before the whole court they swore an oath to each other, and preparations went ahead for the wedding, amid general sorrow for the loss of the brave and handsome knight to one so hideous. Queen Guinevere tried to persuade Ragnell to marry quietly, away from public gaze, but the lady demanded that the ceremony take place in the great church at midday, and that there should be a banquet in the court afterwards. To this the queen assented, though reluctantly, and all was done as Ragnell had requested. Everyone was dismayed at her ugliness, despite the fine dress she wore to be married, and looked in sorrow to see her stand beside the handsome knight. At the feast her manners revolted all who sat near her at the table and she continued eating until there was nothing left. Then bride and groom retired to their bed-chamber.

Once there Ragnell asked if her husband would be as courteous to her in bed as he had been in open court, saying that she knew that if she were beautiful he would not have needed to be asked. She requested a kiss at least. Gawain declared that he would do more than just kiss her, and when he turned to embrace her, he saw the most beautiful woman he had ever seen standing next to him.

'In God's name, what are you?' he asked.

'Sir, I am your wife,' Ragnell replied.

'How can this be?' asked Sir Gawain, and Ragnell told him that she was under an enchantment until she could find a man good enough to marry her even as she had looked before. But the spell was not wholly undone, for there was still a choice Gawain must make. Either he could have her fair by night and foul by day, or the other way about. Gawain agonized for a time over this, but in the end he said that it was for her to choose, since it affected her as much or more than he. At this Ragnell clapped her hands and told him that thus was the spell upon her broken completely. For all that was required was for her to find a man who would give her sovereignty over himself – the answer, indeed, to Gromer's riddle. Such every woman desires most: to be given the right to choose for herself who and what she will be.

In the morning everyone was amazed by the transformation in Ragnell. She and Sir Gawain lived happily together until her death, after which he mourned her for the rest of his life.

This powerful story tells us a great deal about the Loathly Lady or, as she has become here, the Loathly Bride. By seeking to help King Arthur, and by marrying Gawain, she is seeking healing from the spell that has forced her to adopt a hideous exterior. She asks only that she should be given sovereignty, the right to choose for herself who and what she will be; a right that many still seek in vain. Only when Gawain offers her that right is she healed, and he must do so in ignorance of the outcome. It would have been easy for him to impose the form of the Hideous Damsel on her, by day to both their shames, by night to his discomfort. Instead he gives her the gift of choice, finally breaking the spell in which she has been held.

This, surely, is the reason why the Hideous Damsel comes to the court to remind the Wounded Hero to return to his task. She herself is wounded by the distorted image that has been placed upon her, as upon so many women today, by others. Her suffer-

ing is part of the blight upon the land that is in turn the product
of the Fisher King's own wound or, in our own terms, the
damage we have done to the earth. Thus we see how when
the king is healed the land will be healed also and so, in turn,
will Cundry – or Ragnall.

Again, we notice that the crux of the story revolves around
the asking and answering of a question, which here is: 'What is
it women most desire?' The asking of this question, whether it
is addressed to a man (and it should be noted that men can and
do learn a great deal from asking this), or to a woman, which is
something all women need to do at least once in their lives,
results in a healing experience. Ragnell receives the right to be
herself, to heal her own wounds; Gawain is freed of the need to
make the decision for her – he relinquishes his stereotyped role
of dominant male and as a result is set free to acknowledge and
'marry' his feminine self. The mythic argument for this is deep
and complex, and draws us inevitably to look again at the
theme of the Waste Land.

We saw above and again in Chapter 4 that the ruin of
the land is intimately connected to the health or otherwise
of the king. We saw too that according to ancient Celtic
traditions the king actually married the land over which he
ruled, and that this event was symbolically enacted by inter-
course with a woman who represented the land. Her name,
in each case, is given as Sovereignty. She is the sovereign soul
of the land which the king must acknowledge before he is
considered fit to rule. She appears, initially, in a hideous form.
Only when the putative king acknowledges her inner beauty,
and kisses her, does she transform. It is the story of Gawain and
Ragnell again, and this is why the Hideous Damsel uses the word
'sovereignty' in the poem. The original myth may have been
forgotten by the time it was written, but the word still bears its
charge. Gawain is doing more than giving Ragnell 'her own way'
(as the poet Geoffrey Chaucer makes it in his re-telling of the
story in *The Wife of Bath's Tale*). He is acknowledging her wound
and offering her the opportunity to be healed.

It is of course true, that women are perfectly capable of healing
themselves without having to ask permission of a man. But we
need to remember that Ragnell seeks out the man she believes
will be able to help her – there is a quiet confidence about her
every act throughout the poem – even when she is behaving
most brutishly. In addition it is important to remember that

very often the wounds we carry within us result from relationships, both good and bad, and that the best way to heal them lies in a mutual partnership between man and woman. Thus in this story Ragnell offers the only way for Arthur to save his life – to heal his wound – and he must trust her and put himself in the hands of both Gawain and Ragnell in order to do so.

A woman's true nature is her beauty – not just her inner beauty, but her whole being – which is illuminated by her self-respect, her compassion for others, her truth and integrity. As Caitlín Matthews remarks in her book *In Search of Woman's Passionate Soul*(33), 'the process of disenchanting the hag . . . takes the wisdom of the opposite sex to be ultimately effective. Until we are able to recognize each other's authentic selves as the true face, rather than relating to masks of projected femininity or masculinity, how are we to proceed?'(33)

We might notice here that King Arthur's primary wound in nearly all of the myths is represented by the breakdown of his relationship with Guinevere, who loves elsewhere. And that since Guinevere represents the sovereignty of the land for him, this failure is a direct cause of the Waste Land effect within his kingdom. If we accept the possibility – which I believe is implicit within the Arthurian myths – that the Wounded King is a surrogate for Arthur, and that the Waste Land is also the Britain over which he rules, then not only does the story make greater sense, but also the essential theme of mutual respect and mutual healing through love comes sharply to the fore.

To put this into mythic terms, the land is wounded by the failure of the king to retain a right relationship to it, for whatever reason. Arthur and Guinevere are trapped in a destructive relationship with Lancelot, who is also the king's best friend. The links between king and land become severed, the Dolorous Blow is struck and the king (be he Arthur or the Fisher King) is wounded in his generative function (Arthur and Guinevere are childless in the majority of the stories), and the land grows waste. But the soul of the wounded land cries out, and sends its messenger, Cundry, the Hideous Damsel, or Ragnell, to summon the Wounded Hero, Perceval or Gawain, to find his way to the Castle of the Grail and heal the king. His course is a hard one, and he must undergo much pain and suffering before he succeeds. But in the end the land flowers, the wheel turns and life continues. For Arthur and Guinevere it is too late. They have betrayed the trust of the land and a period of darkness will follow until another comes to rule over the land. Even here the myth is consistent; Arthur does not die at the end of the story, but passes to Avalon and enters a long dream of ages until he is called back to rule again, wise in the knowledge of what has been learned in his previous lifetime. Meanwhile, in the heart of the kingdom, a light gleams out. The Waste Land has been healed, the Voices of the Wells restored, and the Court of the Rich Fisherman functions again, awaiting the coming of the next Wounded Hero, who must make the journey of Perceval to find healing.

In human terms, healing requires co-operation on many levels: with our inner selves, with our partners, and with the universe. We can, if we like, internalize all of these as aspects of our unconscious selves, or we can work with the imagery of stories like the ones we have been considering here, externalizing our search for a cure to our sickness. The potential for the cure is always present and discoverable, *if* we have the courage to face our wounds and not give them power over us.

We may recognize and acknowledge our wounded state, but Ragnell or Cundry must still be faced, the Loathly Bride married, if we are to find the depths of positive awareness within us. The Loathly Lady comes to challenge our awareness, and she often berates us with harsh words. But if we can meet with her and give voice to our wounds, we can enter into a meaningful dialogue. Cundry demands that we face up to our innermost fears and that we reach within to discover the answers that are *already there* or, as the myth of *The Elucidation* puts it, recover the Voices of the Wells. Ragnell demands that we look the truth – however ugly – in the eyes and make our response accordingly. We have to acknowledge the problem and deal with it. We have to make ourselves 'one with the land', which represents our lives and the world and our partners and family and friends, because only when our own wounds are acknowledged and healed can we rejoin that world. In terms both of the story and of our personal lives, the Loathly Lady is the voice of the Wounded Land (as the maidens are the Voices of the Wells), and we must let her speak out, relating the truth concerning the wounds of the earth and our own connection with them, before we can properly begin the process of healing.

Exercise 12 The Loathly Lady

In this exercise you will be meeting the Loathly Lady herself, and submitting yourself to her test. This works equally well whether you are a man or a woman. Neither Cundry nor Ragnall know boundaries of gender, and either will present herself in whatever form she needs. Because this encounter is so flexible according to the needs of the individual, it takes the form of a shamanic journey rather than a visualization. The journey will be to the Middleworld, which is an extension of our own dimension but seen as a more real and vital place. Begin from your usual starting place, which you should remember is somewhere familiar to you in this world. Follow the instructions on pp xxi–xxii and 13–16, and call the Questing Beast to accompany and guide you. Ask it to take you to Cundry or Ragnall and, when you are face to face with her, submit yourself to her judgement. She will most certainly be unequivocal and direct, but she is never cruel nor overly harsh. Her judgement may take several forms, aimed at helping you to identify your wounds, and to deal with them, either collectively or singly. She may offer you advice as to how you can undertake the healing and restoration of your missing soul-parts. Or she may simply give you a message or a task to perform in the Otherworld. Be attentive to her words and actions, and when you have completed the journey, if you have not been journeying aloud, write down everything you can remember.

Gawain's Quest

There can be little doubt that the story of Gawain and Ragnell provides some important clues to the story of the Damsels of the Wells. In addition it shows Gawain in a role which demonstrates his true ability in the matter of the Grail Quest. In the orthodox accounts of the quest Gawain is a non-starter. Judged to be too worldly, to love women too much, he is rapidly demoted by the monkish writers of the later works, until there is little to like about him. Yet, this was not always the case, as the story summarized above ably demonstrates. Earlier still, Gawain was regarded as a premier hero of Arthur's court, one who, in the words of an early Welsh account 'never returned without success from any mission he undertook'.

This theme is borne out not only in the story discussed here, but also in the versions of the Grail Quest in which Gawain features more centrally. In most of these he is judged as a failure, but on two occasions he is either wholly or partly

successful. These stories restore Gawain to his rightful place as a leading player in the Grail mysteries, and incidentally add some significant points to the quest for healing.

The inability to recognize the existence of both the masculine and the feminine within us is one of the prime causes of woundedness. This is because the soul, inasmuch as it can be said to possess gender of any kind, contains both and, if one or other aspect is not recognized or honoured, then the soul is out of balance and prone to sickness. In the stories this is frequently expressed in the degree to which the inner masculine and inner feminine are acknowledged or ignored. Thus much of Perceval's adventures have to do with his reconciling his new-found masculinity with his original understanding of the feminine, and it is only when he has done so that he is at last able to perform the act of healing for the Wounded King.

But if Perceval's adventures act out this inner struggle, which ends with the healing of the deep masculine, there is little doubt that a parallel story, concerning the healing of the feminine, is to be found within the stories relating to Gawain. In fact, Gawain's quest for the Grail is very different to that of Perceval, though it nonetheless contains a definite healing story of its own. This is not the place to examine all of the stories which relate to Gawain's career, nor do I wish to reprise the arguments already set forth in my book *Gawain: Knight of the Goddess*(38), in which it is demonstrated that the curious blackening of Gawain's character, which takes place systematically throughout the medieval texts in which he appears, happens because he was associated with the ancient Goddess religion. This association was preserved in the fact that Gawain has relationships with a number of women, but although this was typically represented as lust by the medieval scribes who recorded the stories, Gawain's amorous nature was in fact an expression of his devotion to the Goddess as she is represented by *all* women. As we have seen, this aspect of the myths became polarized around the story of Gawain's relationship to the Loathly Lady, who is herself an aspect of the Hideous Damsel who urges on the knights to seek the Grail. This relationship conforms to that between the king and the land, and shows how when the two are in a harmonious relationship there is no expression of the negative activity found within the Grail romances which feature Perceval. To be sure, Gawain does not always succeed in the quest, but the story of hesitation and failure to ask the questions is largely absent in the accounts of his quest. It is clear that, as someone who already acknowledges and honours the feminine, he is able to see past the problems which beset Perceval.

If this is the case then we are surely correct in seeing Gawain not as a negative version of Perceval, but as someone who learns, through his initiation at the hands of women, how to activate the lost, wounded femininity of his own soul. When he has succeeded in this he is able to bring about the necessary act of healing which, though described in conventional terms in most of the stories, still reflects the very different nature of the two heroes.

In effect Gawain is a far more integrated and complete figure than Perceval. In his childhood he is rejected by his mother and is brought up by strangers. Yet he transcends these initial setbacks and rises to a high place in the court of his uncle, King Arthur. Later he acquires the reputation of a 'ladies' man', as someone who loves lightly and easily and then passes on his way. This is given as the reason for his failure in the quest, despite the fact that he is the first of the Round Table knights to declare that he will not rest until he has found out about the Grail. In fact there is plentiful evidence to suggest that he was, at one time, the original Grail winner, and in at least one account he is depicted as such. In fact, although he is consistently seen to fall in the greatest test of the Arthurian myths, he teaches by example and is, in his own terms, just as successful as Perceval. It is his adventures, particularly with the Loathly Lady, that show the way towards the wholeness which Perceval seeks.

It is surely no accident that, in Chretien's account, we see Gawain entering the Grail Castle by way of the Water Gate, the way of the senses and emotions. In the same way, just as Perceval has most to do with the Grail, most of Gawain's experiences centre around the image of the sword. Both, of course, make use of the spear to perform the act of healing, and we can very clearly see how this is borne out in the symbolism attached to both weapons, and to the Grail itself. Jungian analyst Marion Woodman has written wisely of this in her study of the wounded feminine, *The Ravaged Bridegroom*.

> *The legend makes it clear that the Grail serves the lance, even as the lance serves the Grail. The Grail [as the inner feminine] is raised to a consciousness that is the penetration of the lance, even as the penetration of the lance is the raising of the consciousness of the Grail. The one is present in*

the other, the two are in consciousness indissolubly linked. In the loss of
that organic, life-giving connection between masculinity and femininity
resides the sterility of the Fisher King and the Waste Land over which he
presides.(61)

If we are to restore the neglected part of ourselves – whether, as men, we learn to acknowledge our inner femininity or, as women, we learn to acknowledge our inner masculinity – we have to be prepared to travel out of our usual mind-set into another realm. The next exercise is intended to put us in touch with our emotional selves, and is a polarized experience to that of crossing the Sword Bridge (see Exercise 7).

Exercise 13 The Water Gate

Close your eyes and prepare to set forth on a journey. It is a journey you have taken before and one that you will take again, as often as you need to, until you have healed yourself and found the truth which lies at the heart of the Grail. As your breathing slows and finds its rhythm, and as your consciousness undergoes the change from ordinary to subtle reality, you find that you are, once again, standing on the edge of the stretch of water which separates the land from the island where the Castle of the Grail is like a bright beacon in the light of the noonday sun. To one side lies the Sword Bridge, which you crossed successfully on another visit. But as you look to the other side you see an opening in the earth which you had not noticed before. Rough-hewn stones line the entrance to a dark tunnel which seems to lead towards the castle walls. The smell of damp comes wafting from it as you approach, and you look around in the hope of seeing someone who will tell you whether or not you should enter. But there is no one in sight, and all your innermost senses tell you that this is the path you must take this day . . .

Steeling yourself, you advance slowly down the tunnel, which slopes away at a steep angle, so that you are soon deep under the earth. You feel the walls pressing closely in on either side, and are aware of the rough roof just above your head. Yet, despite the discomfort of the place, you feel surprisingly light and unafraid, as though you had left some kind of weight behind when you entered the tunnel . . .

You lose track of time as you fumble your way even deeper into the earth; then suddenly, somewhere ahead, you see a faint gleam of light. Gradually it increases until you see what seems like firelight dancing on the walls of the tunnel. In another moment you come out into a cavern of considerable size. To one side a fire is burning steadily, its light reflected back from the walls, which are embedded all over with crystalline forms, thousand-faceted as a thousand mirrors. The floor of the cavern slopes away beneath you, and filling the centre is a large pool of still, dark water . . .

As you go forward you become aware of a dark figure sitting huddled beside the fire. As you approach the figure raises its head and you find that you are looking into the dark, seamed and twisted face of the Hideous Damsel. At first you are almost repulsed, but as you force yourself to look into her face, you see that there is one feature that is different from all the rest – her eyes. Clear and deep as the pool at the centre of the cavern, they regard you without fear, or animosity. There is a gentleness and compassion within them that strikes a deep chord within you . . .

The Hideous Damsel indicates that you should sit beside her, and you do so willingly, enjoying the warmth of the fire and her silent presence. And as you sit thus tears come unbidden to your eyes, and with them memory stirs within you. You think back to the last time you felt moved in this way – was it yesterday, or a month past, or even longer? . . . [Pause]

For a time you sit thus, tears running down your cheeks. Then abruptly the Hideous Damsel speaks to you. Her voice is deep and throaty, and she asks you what it is that moves you so deeply. You attempt to tell her, struggling for words perhaps, trying to free the waters of your heart . . . [Pause]

At length, when you are finished, the Hideous Damsel turns her head and looks at you again. Then she reaches out her clawed and withered hand and takes one of your own in hers. Together you rise and walk to the edge of the water. There your clothes fall from you and you walk naked into the pool . . .

The water is cold at first, but soon grows warm. You splash about happily, aware that the dark figure from the cavern is somewhere beside you. As you move deeper into the water a sense of greater and greater freedom rises in you. Even if you have never learned to swim, here you can do so, and the sense of liberation is greater than anything you have felt before. Deep within you feel a dam crumbling, letting forth a tidal wave of long repressed emotion which floods you through and through . . .

Your tears flow swiftly again, mingling with the water of the cavern, and with them go many things: fear of the wounds you bear within you; hatred of those who may have caused them; the dependence on things or people that you have used to keep yourself afloat in your daily life; the sense of your wounds as rafts upon which to cling, identity badges which entitle you to greater consideration and love . . .

All these and more are washed out of you in that released tidal wave of emotion and, as you seem to grow lighter, so you begin, paradoxically, to sink deeper into the water. Yet you feel no panic, only a peaceful lulling of your tired spirit, and you find that you are able to breath easily beneath the water, without fear of drowning . . .

Looking down below the water you become aware of a light shining up towards you, and now you actively seek to get to its source, diving ever deeper through the water, until you burst out, suddenly and surprisingly, back into the cavern . . .

There, waiting for you on the edge of the pool is the figure of the Hideous Maiden. But now as you look up into her face, you see that she has changed, that her face is now fair where before it was foul. She reaches down a slim strong hand and pulls you swiftly out of the water, handing you a warm robe in which to wrap yourself. Together you return to the fire and sit again in companionable silence . . .

After a time the maiden turns towards you, and as you look again into her eyes you see reflected there an image of yourself . . . but transformed! Had you never noticed the dark shadows that lay over your face, that made you seem as ugly as the Hideous Maiden herself? Now that they are no longer there, you recognize them for what they were – the outer signs of the pain and fear and rejection you were holding fast to as if they were lifelong friends. All are washed away in the tidal waters of emotion. You feel suddenly freer and lighter than you can ever remember being . . .

Gently the maiden tells you it is time to depart, and reluctantly you take your leave of her. She takes your hand briefly in hers, then embraces you warmly. 'You may return whenever you wish,' she tells you. 'Be sure that we shall meet again.'

With than you make your way back up the tunnel to the outer world. As you emerge you look back at the walls of the Grail Castle, and see a solitary figure standing there. She raises a hand in farewell, and with that the scene begins to fade . . . You open your eyes and you are back in the place where you began this journey. Take your time to re-establish contact with your normal consciousness, and to note down any realizations you had on this journey. You should expect to feel changed and renewed over the next few days or weeks. Part of you will never be the same, and many of your wounds are no longer empowered to hurt you again.

The Death of the Light

Continuing the theme of Gawain's Grail Quest, we come to two texts which show just how different his Grail experiences are to those of Perceval, and in one of these we see some intriguing parallels to the story of *The Elucidation*.

The late Jessie Weston, one of the foremost Arthurian scholars of her time, believed that the story found in Wauchier's continuation of Chretien's *Perceval* is actually far older than its precursor. Whether this view is correct of not is not important here; what concerns us is the significantly different story of the Grail search that it contains, which makes Gawain, rather than Perceval, almost succeed in achieving the mystery. The story may be summarized as follows:

Arthur arranges to rendezvous with the queen at a certain cross-roads, marked by four pine trees. One evening, while waiting, the queen begins a game of chess. As she is playing, a knight rides past who fails to offer the customary greeting and salutation. Annoyed by this, the queen sends Sir Kay to follow the stranger, but he is easily overthrown. At which point Gawain takes up the challenge and catching up with the knight requests him to return and explain his discourtesy to the queen. The knight explains that he is engaged upon a quest which will brook no delay, but Gawain succeeds in persuading him to come back anyway. As they are riding along together, the knight suddenly falls dying, wounded by a spear cast by an unseen hand. With his dying breath the knight bids Gawain don his armour and take up his quest. The hero, furious at the breach of his safe-conduct, agrees and, leaving the dead body in the care of the queen, sets out at once.

He soon passes the borders of Arthur's kingdom and finds himself in a waste land by the shore of the sea. A causeway, bordered on either side by trees, their roots in water, runs out to sea and in the distance Gawain sees a light. At first he wants to wait until morning, but his steed takes the bit between its teeth and gallops across the causeway. At the other end is a hall, and Gawain is at first greeted as if he were known there. But when he takes off his helmet it is seen that he is a stranger and he is left alone. Entering the hall he sees a bier, on which lies a body draped in silk, with a broken sword on its breast and four censers at the four corners of the bier. A procession enters and vespers for the dead are celebrated amid general lamentation. Gawain sees that on a dais are a lance, fixed upright in a silver socket, from which a stream of blood flows continually into a golden cup and, as it overflows, is carried thence by a narrow runnel out of the hall.

Servants now begin to prepare a meal, and the king of the castle enters and speaks kindly to Gawain. The butlers pour wine into fine cups and there then enters into the hall 'the rich Grail' which serves them without the help of servant or seneschal. Gawain wonders much at this, so that he scarcely dare eat. Then once supper is over, the king leads Gawain to the bier, and handing him the broken sword, asks that he restore it. Gawain tries but fails, and the king is sorrowful and tells him he cannot now succeed in his quest. Nevertheless he has shown valour in coming there and may ask any question he likes. Gawain asks about the lance, and is told that it is the weapon which belonged to Longinus. It is destined to remain

where it is, and to bleed, until Doomsday. Then as the king prepares to tell the story of the broken sword and the dead man on the
bier, Gawain falls asleep. He awakens in the morning to find that he
is alone on the seashore, his horse secured to a rock, while all traces
of the castle have vanished. Wondering greatly, Gawain sets off
through the land, noticing it no longer seems so wasted, and is met
by both blessings and curses: blessings for having asked concerning
the lance, curses for not also asking about the Grail.

There are several important details in this story, not the least of
which is the similarity with the account of the Grail found in
the second part of *The Elucidation*(6), and which therefore
connects it with the story of the Damsels of the Wells, but also
that Gawain is the protagonist, and at least partially successful
at that. We also see that the story of the Dolorous Blow and the
invisible knight who wounds the man with whom Gawain is
travelling are here drawn into the frame. By adding the details
supplied by the Balin story we can identify the wielder of the
spear as Garlon, and it is possible to suggest that the dead man
on the bier may well have been slain by the same invisible
assailant.

In another text, the Maimed King is specifically identified
with Perceval's father, so that he is thus on a quest to heal his
own parents. We may allow ourselves to see in this a reflection
of the wounding relationships which so often exist between
father and son and between parent and child in general. Or we
may see the child as the soul-part which requires healing and
rediscovery if we are to become whole. When set alongside the
story told above, this suggests that at some point Garlon may
have slain either his own brother, or their father, depending on
the identity of the dead king.

This is very interesting since it tells us that the dark side of
the Grail King (whom we have recognized Garlon to be) is
capable of killing his light half. Or if we accept the idea that the
dead king on the bier is the father of Garlon and Pellam (which
would seem to be the case in the light of the evidence supplied
both by this and the other texts) then the son has wounded the
father. These kinds of wounds, which are common to many
parent/child relationships, can only be addressed at a very
deep level, and if not dealt with can cause the kind of Waste
Land effect described in the story.

Of course wounds can be, and often are, inherited. Parents

readily pass on their own wounds to their children. We can see this clearly in the Wounded King story, where his whole family is wounded by being made guardians of the Grail. Sometimes to be given stewardship over something (or someone) can be as damaging as a direct wound, leading to power complexes and manipulative relationships. We are eager to share our wounds with others because we feel alone and because we believe that to pass on the wound to another will somehow rid us of our pain.

However, as one respondent noted, 'I am not the cause of my own wound.' This is an important realization. We can blame ourselves only too easily for the wounds we bear or the wounds we think we have caused others – family, friends, lovers – without ever coming close to seeing the true nature of what wounds us and why – hence our need to question.

Gawain's crossing of the causeway – again, we noticed, over water – shows that his emotional self must be encouraged. He is literally 'carried away' by his steed; his falling asleep before he can learn the reasons for the state of the land and the means by which it can be healed represents that part of us that does not want to be healed at all, but would rather remain in a state of woundedness. This is the part of us which actively wants to be wounded; it looks around and sees that everyone else is wounded and seeks out some grievance and builds it into something more. This is like the figure of the king whom we encountered in Chapter 2, who wounds himself because of the sorrow he feels for the dead knight, or Clingsor, who castrates himself in order to seize the power of the wound for himself. This relates also to the way Pellam attacks Balin for killing Garlon, or Peredur seeks vengeance for the death of his cousin. In both cases the cause of the wound is the vengeance. The long-term effect is even worse: the Fisher King becomes helpless, a prisoner of his woundedness, hence the need for the Wounded Healer, who has already undergone this process and is able to see through the veil of lies and falsification with which the king has surrounded himself.

It is easy to see from this that not everyone wants to be healed. We can become so attached to our wounds – the reason for our inadequacy, failure or dissatisfaction – that we do not want to be rid of them. In another sense, they can actually help us by providing us with the strength to continue, as in the case of one correspondent, who wrote that, 'My wounds are like the fire within the earth – they rescue me from a repose of body and spirit in which I would never do anything remarkable.' The cost of this kind of reliance on the wounded state can be high, though there is a happy medium. We do not need our wounds, but we can learn from them: it is all a question of balance. If we let our wounded state overwhelm us, then we can become as barren and impotent as the Wounded King. If we allow our wounds to educate us, we can begin the active pursuit of healing, just as the earth does by calling forth its own healing agent in Cundry, and as the Wounded King does by attempting to generate his own saviour.

The Weeping Maidens

The second of the stories dealing with Gawain's Grail Quest is the medieval German story *Diu Crone* or The Crown, composed by Heinrich von dem Tulin around 1250(3). It is unique in that it is the only text which makes Gawain a successful Grail winner, and as a story it contains some extremely interesting details.

> After many adventures Gawain arrives on the borders of a land so lovely and so overflowing with goodness that it seems to him a veritable Earthly Paradise. There he sees a building made all of glass, in which anything that passed might be seen by those who passed by. Entrance to this is prevented by a fiery sword, which Gawain deems a sign of ill-omen. Continuing on his way he finds that even simply being in the land makes him feel stronger, so that the pains of his adventures fall away from him. Twelve days into the country he meets with Lancelot and Colgrevance, and having exchanged stories of their adventures they continue on together. Soon after they meet a squire who invites them to accompany him back to his master's castle. They agree and follow the directions given to a fine and rich place where they are made welcome. They enter a hall filled with the finest things, the floor of which is strewn with roses. Their host sits on a throne watching two youths playing chess. He greets the three knights warmly and they all sit down together and exchange light conversation until nightfall, when they are summoned to dine.
>
> A splendid feast ensues, with everything they could possibly want. A great company gathers, many knights and ladies, minstrels and servants to care for their every need. When all are seated a noble youth enters with a great sword which he lays before the

king. Then come others who serve them with meat and drink, though neither the king nor his followers partake of either. Gawain, puzzled by this, also takes no food or wine. His companions, however, being hungry, eat and drink and almost at once fall into a deep slumber. Seeing this Gawain refuses all his host's encouragements to satisfy his hunger and thirst, and keeps himself awake and alert.

Then there comes into the hall a procession, consisting of two maidens with candelabra, two youths who bear between them a spear, a maiden carrying a salver of gold and precious jewels on a silken cloth, and behind them: '. . . treading soft and slow, paced the fairest being whom since the world began God had wrought in woman's wise, perfect was she in form and feature, and richly clad withal. Before her she held on a rich cloth of samite a jewel wrought of red gold, in form of a base, whereon there stood another, of gold and gems, fashioned even as a reliquary that standeth upon an altar. This maiden bore upon her head a crown of gold, and behind her came another, wondrous fair, who wept and made lament, but the others spoke never a word, only drawing nigh unto the host, and bowed them low before him.'(16)

Gawain recognizes the crowned maiden as someone he has met before on his adventures, who had bidden him, when next he saw her, and in the company of five other maidens, not to fail to ask what they did there. He watches as they lay the spear on the table with the salver beneath it, into which, to his wonder, three drops of blood are shed. The reliquary is placed on the table next, and Gawain sees that it contains bread. The old king at once partakes of both this and of the drops of blood, and Gawain can no longer keep silent but prays to know the meaning of these wonders.

Immediately the entire company leaps up, crying aloud in joy until the king bids them keep silent. The noise briefly awakens Lancelot and Colgrevance, but they fall asleep almost at once, at which point the king speaks to Gawain: 'Sir Gawain, this marvel . . . may not be known unto all, but shall be held secret, yet since you have asked thereof, sweet kinsman and dear guest, I may not withhold the truth. This is the Grail which you now behold. Herein have you won the world's praise, for manhood and courage have you right well shown, in that you have achieved this toilsome quest. Of the Grail may I say no more save that you have seen it, and that great gladness has come of this your question. For now are many set free from the sorrow they long had borne, and small hope had they of deliverance. Great confidence and trust had we in Perceval, that he would learn the secret things of the Grail, yet hence did he depart even as a coward who ventured naught, and asked naught. Thus did his quest miscarry, and he learned not that which of a surety he should have learned. So had he freed many a mother's son from sore travail, who live, and yet are dead. Through the strife of kinsmen did this woe befall . . . [and] the living were driven out, but the dead must abide in the semblance of life and suffer bitter woe withal . . . [until] there be a man of their race who should end this their sorrow, in that he should demand the truth of these marvels . . . and they should again enter into joy . . . This spear and this food they nourish me and none other, for . . . dead I am, though I bear not the semblance of death, and this my folk is dead with me . . .' (ibid)

The king explains that though he is dead the maidens are not, but are there to serve him once a year from the Grail. Then he gives Gawain the sword, telling him that it will always serve him well and never break. Then both the king and all his company, save for the maidens, vanish utterly away, and thus is the quest for the Grail ended.

In many ways this is one of the most remarkable stories we have seen. Not only does it look ahead to the eventual state of healing, but it almost certainly contains the true resolution to the story of the Damsels of the Wells.

Once again we have some remarkable variations on the theme. The King (who is not described as wounded, but who suffers from the deepest wound of all) together with his court, with the exception of the five maidens, are all dead, and can only be released by the asking of the question. Once Gawain does so all express their deep joy, a detail which, as we shall see in Chapter 6, is of great importance, since it refers to the final healing of all wounds. Death here takes the place of the unhealing wound, and can be seen as referring to the general death of the spirit. This itself comes about as a result of a deep wounding of the soul, which nevertheless keeps some part of itself alive in the hope of receiving healing.

The weeping maidens are referred to in several versions, and represent those parts of the soul which cry out for release or recovery and healing. In an interpolation within one manuscript only, the king mentions that among the results of the successful achievement of the quest is that the hero will be given to understand *why* the maidens weep. Although this denouement is never given, it is my belief that at some stage in the development of the story, the achieving of the Grail was seen to have the effect of healing the weeping women. If this is so then we have a direct connection to the Damsels of the Wells, whose tears are able to flow when the Court of the Rich Fisherman is discovered – the difference between tears of joy and tears of sorrow being negligible in the effect they have on the wounds of those who shed them. Certainly this makes a fitting resolution to the story begun in *The Elucidation*, which despite its current ending is unsatisfactory since it leaves so much unsaid. With the ending provided by *Diu Crone* we have a working out of the myth in a way that speaks to us all. The joy described is palpable; the dead are released into greater life.

In this version there is no Waste Land, but rather an earthly paradise which actually heals those who journey within it. Instead there is the strange glass house protected by a blazing sword. The meaning of this remains obscure; however, it is possible to see it as the 'holding-cell' in which many of those who are wounded place themselves, throwing away the key and remaining inside thereafter, until someone comes to shatter the walls. For those who occupy this place, it is perfectly possible to see out, and to continue living an outwardly normal life; and those who are outside can see in just as easily, often perceiving the wounds of those who live within but being unable to reach them. This is the Waste Land in which so many of us live out our whole lives, waiting for the healer who sometimes never comes. Gawain is uneasy both because he perceives it as excluding privacy, and because it is empty, as though those who once dwelled within had been spirited away by an unknown agency. In reality it is that very emptiness, that desolation and separation which is both the root and the outward expression of so many wounds in the soul of the individual. The soul feels unaccountably fearful when it recognizes that something is wrong but cannot understand what. The great unasked question awaits the hero at this point; he must overcome his sense of unease before he can ask it. And as we have repeatedly seen throughout our examination of these stories, it is most often a woman, the feminine part of the soul, that shows the way. Here Gawain sees the crowned maiden and recognizes her as someone who once spoke to him of the Grail: the feminine part of his soul reminds him that there is a task to perform, and when he does so healing occurs.

Behind all of this lies a deeper message, one which involves both personal and individual healing, the ravishing of the land and, ultimately, the restoration of inner beauty to the soul, which as we have seen is often reflected outward by the wounds we bear. We have seen how Gawain and Ragnell, by uniting, express the restoration of the earth and the healing of the wounded feminine. In following Gawain's quest we have seen how, as the Knight of the Goddess, he is able to recognize the sovereignty of the land and of women and achieve the mystery of the Grail. In the final chapter we shall begin to bring together the many themes which we have explored on our journey together, and make of them a vehicle for that restoration.

6 The Courts of Joy

Then Geraint went and sounded the horn. And at the first
blast he gave, the mist vanished. And all the hosts came
together, and they all became reconciled to each other.

The Mabinogion Geraint ab Erbin

EREC AND ENIDE

The final chapter in our quest for healing takes us deep into the
strange and wonderful world of Celtic myth and legend, specifically where it touches upon the Arthurian tradition. It is here
that we find the last few links in the story which point the way
to the healing of the Wounded King, which in this context is
referred to as 'the restoration of the Courts of Joy'.

In *The Elucidation* the object of King Arthur's knights is to find
the whereabouts of the Court of the Rich Fisher, 'from whence
shall come the joy whereby the land shall again be made
bright'. According to the story-teller Master Blihis, only then
will the Voices of the Wells be restored and the power of the
Grail be released to heal both the king and the land. To answer
this reference fully we need to look at one more story, that of
Erec and Enide (7), another work by Chretien de Troyes, author
of the original Grail text. We will also look at its Celtic counter-
part, *Geraint ab Erbin* (11), which contains some interesting
variations.

The first half of the story establishes Erec as a brave and
worthy champion, who avenges an insult offered to the person
of Queen Guinevere, and wins for himself a lovely wife named
Enide. He then returns home, and assumes the stewardship of
his own lands in place of his ageing father. Content with his lot,
he no longer rides forth in search of adventure, but remains at
home. His nobles begin to feel unhappy about this and speak of

it to Enide. She, concerned for her lord, wakes one morning and weeps aloud for the loss of his prowess. Hearing her, Erec leaps to the conclusion that she is crying because she loves another, and in a rage sets forth again in quest of adventure, forcing Enide to ride before him in the same ragged dress and to keep silent no matter what she sees or hears.

Further adventures follow, in which the patient Enide suffers all kinds of slights, while remaining steadfastly faithful to Erec. Finally they arrive in the domain of Evrain, a nobleman who has established Enchanted Games in which all comers must participate, or be killed. These games take place in a garden hidden behind a hedge of mist and a fence of stakes on which are set the heads of those who have tried and failed. There are only two empty stakes left.

Erec determines to try his luck, despite Evrain's reluctance; he admires his guest so much that he wishes he had not instituted the games at all. Erec enters the enchanted garden, and the description of what follows is best told in words of the original, in this case the Celtic version, as translated by Lady Charlotte Guest. Here Erec bears the older Celtic name of Geraint. The story follows Chretien's exactly.

> *Then fearlessly and unhesitatingly Geraint dashed forward into the mist. And on leaving the mist he came to a large orchard; and in the orchard he saw an open space, wherein was a tent of red satin; and the door of the tent was open, and an apple tree stood in front of the door of the tent; and on a branch of the apple tree hung a huge hunting horn. Then he dismounted, and went into the tent; and there was no one in the tent save one maiden sitting in a golden chair, and another chair was opposite to her, empty. And Geraint went to the empty chair, and sat down therein. 'Ah! chieftain,' said the maiden. 'I would not council thee to sit in that chair.' 'Wherefore?' said Geraint. 'The man to whom that chair belongs has never suffered another to sit in it.' 'I care not,' said Geraint, 'though it displease him that I sit in the chair.' And thereupon they heard a mighty tumult around the tent. And Geraint looked to see what was the cause of the tumult. And he beheld without a knight mounted upon a war-horse, proudly snorting, high mettled, and large of bone; and a robe of honour in two parts was upon him and upon his horse, and beneath it was plenty of armour.*

The inevitable combat follows, and Geraint is the winner. As his opponent lies wounded on the ground he begs Geraint to spare him. Geraint agrees, on condition that the enchanted games are ended and the hedge of mist dispersed. The fallen knight agrees and instructs Geraint to blow the hunting horn that hangs on the apple tree, which can only be sounded by the one who has succeeded in defeating him. 'Then Geraint went and sounded the horn. And at the first blast he gave, the mist vanished, and all the hosts came together, and they all became reconciled to each other.' Geraint (Erec) and Enid (Enide) are also reconciled, and return home to his lands where they live happily together and where Geraint's 'warlike fame and splendour lasted with renown and honour both to him and Enid from that time forth'.

Sovereignty's Games

Thus ends the story, rather hurriedly one might think, and certainly with a great deal unexplained. Who, for example, is the maiden in the red tent who sits on a chair of gold; why were the Enchanted Games established in the first place; and who is the fearsome challenger whom Erec-Geraint defeats? Much of this can be unravelled by comparing details within the story with episodes gleaned from elsewhere within the rich harvest of the Arthurian tradition. We have already met the maiden before, in more than one guise; she is none other than the Lady Sovereignty, whose other face is that of the Loathly Lady. The Enchanted Games are really a microcosmic re-statement of the hero's entire path, compressed into this single moment. And as to the identity of the challenger, Chretien gives him the name Mabonagrain, which is so charged with mythic significance that it leads us into a whole new area of symbolic reference.

But let us take a step back. This was Chretien's first work, and like his last it has a curious unfinished feel. There are also some remarkable parallels between *Erec and Enide* and *Perceval* (14). Erec's treatment of Enide, forcing her to ride before him in a ragged dress, precisely echoes the fate of the Maiden of the Tent, whose lord misread her encounter with the innocent Perceval as a betrayal and punishes her accordingly. Enide, like Perceval, is instructed never to speak of anything she sees, even when this involves potential danger of which she might have forewarned him. Thus, just as Perceval is prevented from asking the all-important question, so Enide is prevented from taking action to protect or save the man she loves.

Mabonagrain, the challenger, and Evrain (or Owein as he is called in the Welsh version), who is the master of the Enchanted

Games, are both of Otherworldly origin. The former derives the first part of his name from Mabon, the wondrous child-god or *puer eternis* of Celtic tradition; the latter is familiar from various other stories, in one of which he commands a flock of Otherworldly ravens. His castle is called Brandigan – Raven's Castle – which in turn suggests an association with Bran the Blessed, whom as we saw is himself a precursor of the Wounded King. This is simply an earlier incarnation of the story with which we have been working all along, though it reveals some new levels of woundedness.

Both Mabonagrain and Evrain are to be seen as emanations of the dark opponent, or as it is sometimes referred to the 'shadow' side of our own nature, which must be faced and dealt with before we can be wholly cured of our wounds. Like all the Anti-Grail kings we have encountered these are not necessarily negative in themselves, but may take on the form of some un-regenerate aspects of our wounded self in order to draw attention to themselves. Even the darkest and most secret aspects of our woundedness want to be healed at base, and though they may take more effort than our superficial hurts, they will respond to our efforts in time.

The Enchanted Games take place in an ante-chamber of the Otherworld. The presence of the hedge of mist, the fence with stakes and their grisly decoration, the apple tree with the horn hanging upon it, and lastly the identity of the challenger, are all borrowed from Celtic tradition. When Geraint enters he is leaving this world behind and entering another level of reality, where he encounters the mysterious woman in the golden chair. The fact that the place is surrounded by a hedge of sharpened stakes is particularly relevant to our own recognition of our wounded state. Around our own inner wasteland we often build thorn hedges, as thick as those around Sleeping Beauty's castle. Within we lie dormant, barren and empty, waiting the coming of the Healer. This is the wound of isolation, and the only cure is to break down the hedge by engaging with what lies without, by asking the question, which here might be: 'Why have I isolated myself? How can I re-engage with the world again?'

In the story of *Erec and Enide* the person enclosed within the hedge is really Lady Sovereignty, she who represents the inner soul of the land, and who possesses a special relationship to the king. Sovereignty possesses the power of bestowal, and if we recall the story of *Baile in Scail* (The Phantom's Prophecy), which we discussed in Chapter 4, we will remember how the hero, Conn, is abducted to the Otherworld, there to be shown a vision of his kingly destiny:

> They went into the house and saw a girl seated in a chair of crystal, wearing a golden crown. In front of her was a silver vat with corners of gold. A vessel of gold stood beside her and before her was a golden cup. They saw the Phantom himself on his throne . . . 'My name is Lug . . . and I have come to tell you the span of your sovranty . . .' The girl was the Sovranty of Ireland and she gave food to Conn . . . When she went to serve the ale, she asked to whom the cup of red ale [Dergflaith, or red lordship] should be given, and the Phantom answered her 'for Conn'.(20)

In the context of our own search for healing, Sovereignty, the Lady in Red, the Hideous Damsel and the Damsels of the Wells are all images of the inner impulse which prophesies our eventual cure and the ways in which we can seek it. To be given the Red Drink of Lordship is to receive a draught of the healing to come. In the next exercise you will be given the opportunity to do this, and to face a primal fear.

Exercise 14 The Dark Oppressor

In this exercise you are a knight, rather like Perceval, who is engaged on an adventure. It is important to understand that you may take on this role regardless of gender. The role of the knight is simply that of someone who takes on a quest, who faces dangers and gives all that he, or she, can to achieve the tests and trials encountered. Genderal nouns can therefore be ignored for the purposes of this visualization. In this instance the theme of opposition, which we have encountered in the form of Amangons, Garlon and Clingsor, becomes focused in a way that makes it accessible to our own response and we must make a decision as to how we deal with this opponent.

Prepare yourself to go on a journey into the inner realms of the soul . . . Close your eyes and as your consciousness shifts, you find yourself on a high and desolate moorland, across which the wind blows harsh and chill. You are dressed as a knight, with armour and weapons of steel, and mounted upon a spirited charger . . . As you look about you, you see coming towards you another mail-clad figure, armoured all in black, and riding a black horse . . . A shiver of fear runs through you, remembering all those other black knights of whom you have heard. But you turn your horse's head and draw your sword in readiness to fight . . .

Long before the Black Knight is near enough for you to encounter, he reins in his mount and looks towards you. At once you feel yourself caught in an invisible web of power and are unable to move so much as a finger . . . Your sword falls from your nerveless hand and terror overwhelms you, followed almost at once by a sense of calm. Into your mind comes the image of those who have helped you before – the Healer, the Hermit and the Hideous Maiden. Each one is smiling at you, encouraging you to feel no fear . . .

You wait calmly as the Black Knight rides up, and taking the bridle of your horse leads you away . . . In a few moments you are outside the gates of his bleak castle, which open to his command. You enter and your captor leads you to a narrow door in the wall of a grim building . . . Suddenly you are able to move again, but the Black Knight makes it clear that you should do as he commands or else face the consequences. He bids you dismount and enter the door, which swings open at his touch. Within all is dark and dank, and you have to make an effort not to be afraid. The door clangs shut behind you and you are alone in the dark . . .

Gradually your sight clears and you look around, finding that you are in a stone-walled cell with only one barred window, high up in the wall. Fears of being shut in and forgotten rise in you, but once again the faces of your helpers are there to reassure you. You take off your armour and lie down in the straw which covers the floor . . .

You lose track of time and are never sure how long you remain in the dungeon. But there comes into your mind the image of an old, deep wound that you have harboured within you for a long while . . . In this place, without distraction, but not without hope, you can face this wound and ask for healing to be granted to you . . . Spend a while in contemplation of this . . . [Pause]

In a while you hear the door opening and look up to see the Black Knight's faceless helmet. At once he beckons you to follow . . . You hesitate, but feel an inner urge to go forward, and you follow your captor out into the courtyard of the castle . . . There, seated in a golden chair, is a woman dressed all in red. Her face is sternly beautiful and you feel that you are in the presence of a judge. She beckons you forward to stand before her, and the Black Knight matches you step for step.

Something prompts you to look at your captor, and as you do so, he removes his black helmet. You look upon the face of your opponent for the first time, and see with a shock that the face you see is your own . . .

As you stand thus in wonder and fear, the throned Lady addresses you, demanding: 'Which of you is real?'

Your immediate response is to say that it is you who are real, that the other is false, but as you look into the face of the Black Knight you are suddenly uncertain. Is this not really an image of you, this being encased in a carapace of black metal, or is it some monster who has stolen your appearance for its own purpose? You feel a flood of emotions – anger, fear, and doubt – which seem as though they will overwhelm you . . . But for the third time you see the faces of your helpers, and into your mind comes the thought that this question is unanswerable – by you. You turn back to the Lady and tell her that you cannot answer her. Then, placing all your faith in the wisdom of your helpers, you add that you will submit to her judgement . . .

For a moment nothing happens. Then the Lady rises to her feet and comes to stand before you. She looks briefly into your eyes, then turns to the Black Knight. As she looks at him, his armour suddenly begins to fall away. When it is gone he is dressed as you are, so that it is impossible to tell you apart. But the Lady in Red now takes your hand and places it in the hand of your double . . . You want to pull away, but force yourself not to . . .

As you stand thus, linked to this other self, it slowly begins to fade. The last glimpse you have is of that other face – which is your own face – yet softened and somehow changed. Then it has gone, and you feel that something has changed within you.

The Lady has seated herself again, but now she offers you a cup from which to drink. This she tells you, is the Red Drink of Lordship, which re-establishes the sovereignty of the soul within. To drink it is to be blessed with the knowledge of your own heart's truth . . .

Drink now and listen to the song that is for you alone and which springs from deep within your own soul . . . [Pause]

When you are done, take your leave of the Lady. She blesses you as you prepare to depart, and the last you see is her face, its stern lines softened somewhat, so that you are able to see a resemblance to the helpers whom you have met during your inner journeys . . . Slowly you return to normal consciousness, and assess the meaning of your experience with the Black Knight.

As we have seen, the connection between Sovereignty and the king is doubly important, not only for the link it establishes between the king and the land, but also because of the inner relationship of the masculine and feminine aspects of the human soul. The loss of sovereignty equates with a loss of the creative instinct, with the imaginative faculty which makes us uniquely human. The significance of the theft of the golden cups, which appears in *Perceval* (14), in *The Elucidation* (5), and in *Erec and Enide* (7) is an outward manifestation of this. In terms of the soul-life of an individual, it means a loss of power, of certainty, of focus. In all these examples the cup of the inner life is stolen, but it can just as easily be given away, as so often happens in destructive relationships or co-dependency. In all these instances the cup must be won back, rescued from the clutches of its inappropriate keeper. It is here that the wounded-hero-healer enters the picture. Perceval restores the mysterious Grail to is proper function, and redeems the spear by using it to heal the wound it had caused. In *The Elucidation* Arthur's knights set forth with the intention of restoring the Court of the Rich Fisherman, in *Erec and Enide* the hero, who is wounded by his treatment of Enide, overcomes the dark, opposing champion in the Enchanted Games, then blows the royal horn which not only restores the Courts of Joy, but also heals his wounds, and wins back the lost sovereignty of the land and with it the sovereignty of Enide, which Erec had denigrated with his unreasoning behaviour. The pattern is complete in each instance.

- Loss of sovereignty, loss of power, loss of the creative instinct, are all manifestations of woundedness.
- The coming of the wounded-hero-healer, and his long journey, are the first signs of the healing to come.
- The recovery of the sovereignty of self and land; the healing of the outer and inner wounds; the restoration of the Waste Land, of the individual soul, and the Courts of Joy, bring the search for wholeness to completion.

The similarities between the scene in *Baile in Scail* and the encounter of Erec-Geraint are obvious. In the latter the woman in the tent does not have a golden cup or vessels of gold and silver, but these are replaced by the presence of the great hunting horn, which the hero must blow to announce the Joy of the Court. The presence of this object is yet another link in the chain of mythological references which lead towards the triumphant restoration of the Wounded King.

The Royal Horn

Celtic tradition abounds in horns which, when blown, bring about a wondrous event. Bran the Blessed, an early representative of the Wounded King archetype, possesses a magical horn which is something like a cornucopia, providing sustenance for vast numbers of people, as the Grail itself is said to do. In *Erec and Enide* a degree of confusion arises from the variety of spellings and applications used to refer to the horn. If spelled *li cors* it can mean either 'horn' or 'body', but if it is spelled *la cors* it means 'court'. This means that the phrase *joie de li cors* can be read as:

- joy of the court
- joy of the body
- joy of the horn

Thus the Joy of the Court (*la cors*), announced by the blowing of a horn (*li cors*) celebrates the release of the imprisoned Mabonagrain, and at the same time announces the joy of the body (*li cors*). In the context of the themes relating to the Wounded King, the underlying meaning of this is uncannily accurate. The recovery and restoration of the broken soul, the individual wholeness of the hero/king, is indeed expressed by the Joy of the Court and in the joy of the physical body. In all the versions of the story the Wound of the Fisher King is sexual. Only when the pierced thighs of the king (be he Bran the Blessed or Pelles) are healed, is Perceval's long sojourn in the wilderness over, setting him free to marry and celebrate the joy of the body and the joy of the court. The argument is wonderfully circular, telling us as it does that all flesh is blessed, ensouled, and worthy of healing. It is also the perfect coda for our own ongoing quest.

This is borne out even further in the later Grail romances, in which the Fisher King's castle is invariably called either Corbyn or Corbenic. This name can be seen to derive from either *corps beneit* (Blessed Horn) or *corps beneiz* (Blessed Body), and much has been made of this by various commentators. The Blessed Horn is almost certainly a reference to the Royal Horn of Bran; while the Blessed Body is a clear reference to the sacred food of the Christian Eucharist. Both are statements of the transformed body, the Joy of the Court.

The suggestion has also been made that the name derives from *cor-arbennig* which can be read as 'The Sovereign (or Privileged) Chair'. In other words the Throne of Sovereignty, which belongs as much to the Loathly Lady, to the Damsels of the Wells, to the Grail Princess, or to Maiden of the Tent. This all leads one to believe that the castle to which Erec and Enide come, and which is supposedly the home of Evrain-Owein, may actually belong to the Fisher King – or at least to the guardian of a secret so important that it requires a formidable test of skill and bravery to access it, such as the Royal Horn of Bran or the

Cup of Sovereignty, which are both aspects of the Grail. But the test which the young hero undergoes is not simply one of courage and physical strength. It requires a deeper awareness of the state of loss and woundedness in which both hero and king, healer and sufferer are held. The result, if the hero succeeds in overcoming all opposition – which may come from within himself just as easily as it comes from outer opponents – is both in the healing of the wound which has opened between himself and Enide, and in the ending of the Enchanted Games, which in turn has the effect of releasing the reigning champion, Mabonagrain, from the bonds which hold him within the magical garden. The significance of this goes much further, and necessitates a brief look at the myth of Mabon.

The Youthful Prisoner

All that is actually known of what must, at one time, have been an important myth, comes from the story of 'Culhwch and Olwen' in the *Mabinogion* collection(10). The hero, Culhwch, is given a number of seemingly impossible tasks to enable him to win the hand of a giant's daughter. One of these tasks is to rescue Mabon, son of Modron, who was 'taken from his mother when two nights old, and it is not known where he now is, or whether he is living or dead'. With the help of Arthur's warriors and a number of animal helpers, each one older than the rest, Culhwch establishes that Mabon was stolen away immemorial ages ago, and that he has remained in prison ever since. Only the oldest of the ancient animals remembers where the prisoner is held.

When Culhwch and his helpers find their way to the drear castle on a rock beneath which the prisoner is kept they hear a voice which says 'It is Mabon, son of Modron, who is here imprisoned, and no imprisonment was ever so grievous as mine . . .' They free him and continue on to the next task. But though it is buried amid a vast infrastructure of mythic reference and adventure, there is no denying the importance of the release of Mabon, without whose help the remainder of the tasks cannot be accomplished.

This is a profound mystery. The rescue of the god of youth and imagination is a parallel to the winning of the lost symbols of Sovereignty. The hero reaches the castle or the orchard where

these things will be accomplished: he wields the spear that wounds and heals and gives the drink of life from the Grail or the Horn. The prize in each case is healing, the freeing of the waters, the restoration of the Courts of Joy.

Thus in this release from a lifetime of imprisonment we may see a concomitant of the freeing of the Fisher King from his wound. Mabon is, essentially, the god of youth and wonder, worshipped in the Celtic world as Maponus. In the words of the great Mabinogion scholar W. J. Gruffydd, 'Mabon is not only the Great Prisoner, he is also the Immemorial Prisoner, the Great Son who has been lost for aeons and is at last found'. (31). To rescue Mabon is to rescue our own lost youth; to heal the wounds we received in childhood, where so many of us suffer the first blows to the spirit which can accompany us throughout the rest of our lives. Seeking out Mabon, the lost child within, is therefore one of the most urgent of the hero's tasks. The result is the re-establishment of the Courts of Joy, which entails the healing of all wounds, both to the individual and the planetary soul.

The Mabon story is also one of the clearest memorials of the Celtic shamanic tradition, in which a mortal is helped by spirits in animal form. The theme which has shadowed us throughout this book comes to the fore here. Nature, in the form of animal or spirit, comes to our aid, knowing that when we are healed, it is also. The planet possesses an eternal youthfulness which is reflected in the presence of its healing waters, the Wells which go deep into the earth and connect us with the soul of the planet. If we think of Mabon as part of that soul, an emanation of that timeless energy which can both heal and change us, we shall not be far wrong.

The following exercise is a guided visualization to free the Mabon locked within us all. Towards the end there is a pause, at which point you will be prompted to assess your progress so far. Do not be concerned if you do not complete this journey the first time. It is a deep inner voyage to the source of your beginning.

Exercise 15 Releasing the Mabon

Prepare yourself for a journey. Breathe deeply and close your eyes. Let the sense of the place where you are fade into the background and the reality of the vision you see come to the fore. . .

You are standing on the bank of a wide, swift-flowing river. The sun is shining overhead, but there are dark clouds gathering on the horizon. As you look around you see a figure coming towards you. It is a young woman dressed in a flowery robe. Her feet are bare and as you look back along the way she has come, you see that she has left a track of white footprints on the earth; footprints made of white flowers that spring up where she walks. As she approaches she smiles at you, and greets you in a gentle voice. 'I am Olwen, called White Track, the beloved of Culhwch. Welcome to this land.'. You respond with your own greeting, though if the truth be known you feel somewhat overawed in the presence of such fresh beauty.

Olwen turns to look upstream to where, in the distance, you can see a great rock looming out of the land. A huddle of dark buildings is clustered at its top, and there is a feeling of menace about the whole place which makes you uncomfortable. Olwen turns to you and asks: 'Will you help me?' Of course you agree, for how could you not? Olwen explains that her beloved Culhwch is away with the warriors of Arthur, searching for the great boar Twrch Twyth, as well as helping him to achieve other tasks which will enable him to win her hand in marriage. But they have forgotten one task, and this Olwen must accomplish, either alone or with your help. 'We must rescue Mabon,' she says. 'He that was stolen from his mother's side before he was two nights old. Only he can help Culhwch with his greatest task. Will you help me rescue him?'

You agree to do everything you can, and ask where the prisoner is kept, though you already believe you know the answer. Nor are you surprised when Olwen turns towards the grim outcrop of rock far up the stream. 'How shall we get there?' you ask. Olwen points towards the fast-flowing river. And, as she does so, the waters part and a sleek brown head appears. The whiskered face of an otter looks quizzically up at you, and seems in some way to converse with Olwen, who laughs and bids you climb onto the creature's back. 'Do not fear,' she says, 'Otter will carry you safely for part of the way. Another will await you.'

Now you realize that you must undertake this quest alone. 'You will know what to do when you get to the rock,' says Olwen. 'Have faith in your abilities and you will not fail.' Not without trepidation you wade into the swift-flowing river, feeling the water snatch at you, and with difficulty climb onto the back of the Otter, who seems in some way to grow (unless you have shrunk). Clinging to its sleek fur, you are whisked away upstream with surprising speed.

The water splashes into your face and you are forced to close your eyes. You feel intense cold, and yet no sense of fear. The Otter swims strongly and easily, as if the current was nothing to it. Then, in what seems no more than a few moments, you feel the fury of the water lessen, and opening your eyes find that the Otter has swum into a shallow pool cut into the bank of the river. Here, as you look up, you see a mighty Stag, with vast branching antlers, waiting there. Into your mind comes the thought that this is your next helper, and giving thanks to the Otter, you climb out of the river and onto the Stag's back.

At once you are away. You feel the Stag's powerful muscles under you. It covers the ground in a tireless stride, and you look out from between the widespread antlers with an ever-increasing feeling of wonder. In no time at all, it seems, you find yourself at the bottom of a steep slope, and realize you are at the foot of the formidable rock where Mabon is held prisoner. As the Stag comes to a halt, you look up at the frowning face of stone and wonder how you will ever get to the top. Then you hear a high call, the cry of an Eagle, and in a flash of brown and gold the mighty bird descends, alighting on a nearby out-crop of rock. Can this be your next helper? Suddenly you understand that this is so, and you climb down from the Stag's back; having thanked it for its help, you approach the great bird, which stares at you haughtily from its great golden eyes.

As you draw near the Eagle spreads its great wings, and you under-stand that you must mount on the back of this most fearsome of steeds if you are to accomplish your task. The Eagle is truly larger than any you have ever seen, and as you settle yourself on its back you feel a momentary sense of panic. Then the mighty creature rises into the air, and you are filled with wonder as the earth falls away beneath you and the grim face of the rock spins dizzily past. But in a matter of moments the Eagle lands on a narrow shelf of rock, several hundred feet above the ground, and there you see a dark opening in the face of the rock. Descending from the Eagle's back you give it thanks for its help, and then slowly approach the mouth of the cave.

It is intensely dark within, and you wish you had a light. But you press forward anyway, following a tunnel which slopes gently down-ward. In a relatively short time the darkness of the cave gives way to a dim glow of light, which you see emanates from a window in the rock high above. By its poor illumination you see that you are in a small, roughly circular chamber, cut from the living rock. In the centre is a small pool of dark water, but your eyes are drawn not to this, but to an opening in the further side of the cavern. Thick bars of iron are set into the stone, closing it off from either entrance or exit. Behind you sense another chamber, even smaller than this one, and within it there is a slight movement.

Straining your eyes, you cross the cavern and peer in through the gates. In the dim light you can see where a figure stands, and as it senses you it moves closer to the grating. Your eyes meet the eyes of the figure and a shock runs through you. Deep and dream-laden, these are eyes that have seen everything in your world and much more beside, but which are full of love and truth. The face of the pris-oner is one of unearthly beauty, and you are filled with awe as you look upon it. There can be no doubt that this is Mabon, whom you have come to rescue. And with this realization a warm glow enters your heart, and into your mind come words that tell you that you must break down the bars if Mabon is to be set free.

You stare at the thick rods of iron, wondering how you can possibly move them with your puny strength. Then, unbidden, there comes to your mind the realization that the power of love is strong enough to break any bonds, and that if you care enough about the plight of the prisoner, nothing will prevent you from achieving what you have come there to do. You think again of the beautiful Olwen, and as you look into the eyes of Mabon, you are filled with the desire to help. Focus all that desire and strength into a diamond of light, and will the iron bars away . . . [Pause].

When you have done, look up again and see the Mabon step forth into the dim radiance of the cave. His own light now begins to shine forth, adding its warm glow to that cold place. Looking deeply into your eyes he takes your hand and in that moment a dance of joy begins in your heart and spreads through your whole being. You remember nothing of the journey back to the mouth of the cavern, but there the Eagle awaits you and humbly stretches out his wings and bows his glorious head in honour of the Mabon. You both climb onto the great bird's back and in a moment the dark shadow of the rock falls away beneath you. The glory of the land is spread out beneath you, and now you can look down without fear of falling. The mere presence of the Mabon makes everything seem lighter somehow, and you remember your fears with wonder.

In a moment the Eagle descends to the earth, and you find yourself alighting in the midst of a bright garden, full of the scents of flowers and loud with birdsong. There you stand before Mabon, and his true glory is revealed at last. His radiance streams out like a torch in that place, seeming to dim even the light of the sun. It may be that you cannot quite look upon him, nor quite see him fully, but your whole being is filled with the glory of his presence. And there, as you stand in the garden, Mabon gives you a gift, his thanks to you for rescuing him. The gift is the memory of your childhood, healed and cleansed of all darkness, seen as it should always have been seen – in the light of joy. And there is another gift, a lost or missing soul-part, something of yourself which had been lost or mislaid in the past, perhaps again in your childhood or adolescence, where Mabon watches and dreams for you. As he breathes upon you, you feel that lost part re-enter the place where it was always meant to be, and a new sense of harmony flows through you.

You give thanks in whatever way you can, and Mabon blesses you. As his light falls upon you one last time, the scene slowly begins to fade, and you awaken to find yourself returned to your own place and time. But you are changed by what you have seen, and the newly recovered soul-part flutters within you and shines with a bright gleam of the god's light.

Take your time to write down anything you need to from this exercise, and re-establish contact with your usual state of consciousness.

A NEW MYTH OF THE WOUND

This is a primal cleansing that washes away the hurts and wounds of childhood. With it we have almost reached the end of our journey in search of healing. The last pieces of the puzzle are ready to fall into place, and the final story of the Wounded King – which is our own, inner story – can be told.

When all the fragments, gleaned from the many sources we have been examining, are put together, we arrive at a mythic story that is new but which combines elements of all the extant versions. It is offered here as a single pattern of reconstruction which could be put together in a dozen different ways. It should not be regarded as in any way definitive, but as a jumping-off point for your own journey. If we consider it in this light, we will see how well it fits our own situation, and how even in this most desperate of times, there is still hope. A solution to our own wounded state, as well as those wounds that exist within the cosmos, is offered here. It is up to us whether we accept that offer, and follow this particular road to healing, or whether we seek other solutions. As long as we do not give up, accept the situation as inevitable and give power to our wounds, that opportunity will continue to exist. This, then, is a *new* myth of the Wounded King, but one which utilizes all the elements of the old myth, merely drawing forth the meaning hidden within.

The Story of the Wounded Land

In the beginning there are a number of sacred places within the land, which maintain its health and keep open the ways between the worlds. These are the Wells, and each one is inhabited by a female guardian who offers hospitality and refreshment to all who come that way. These women hold the keys to the Otherworld and are able to pass within at will, returning with words of wisdom and healing. They are also the guardians of the sovereignty of the land, to whom all new kings must go in search of blessing and recognition.

For many years all is well, until the appearance of a king named Amangons, who seeks to steal the power of the Wells for himself. He rapes one of the guardians, and steals her golden cup, the symbol of her guardianship, encouraging his followers to do the same. Thus the Voices of the Wells are lost, and the harmony which had existed between the Otherworld and the Land is broken. The soul of the Land itself is damaged, and a veil of enchantment and disempowerment lies over it from that moment onward.

Time passes and King Arthur reigns over the Land. His own relationship to the principle of sovereignty is established on uncertain ground, as is witnessed by his failure to acknowledge his queen as the representative of his own inner sovereignty. He establishes the Fellowship of the Round Table, whose numbers are dedicated to fighting evil wherever it appears. Thus Arthur and his knights attempt to put right the damage that has befallen the Land, but they can only do so much. Then, one day, they encounter the descendants of the Guardians of the Wells in the forest and learn of their history. All declare that they will do whatever they can to help restore the Land to its former health, and are told that only when one of them discovers the Court of the Rich Fisher, and a mysterious treasure which is kept there, will the enchantments be lifted.

Soon after this a knight called Balin le Sauvage stumbles into the Castle of the Rich Fisherman while pursuing an evil murderer named Garlon, a descendent of the king who had caused the wounding of the Land. Balin slays him and in the subsequent battle wounds the current guardian of the place with a magical spear, one of the hallowed treasures kept there. The effect of the wound brings a deepening of the enchantments on the land, which becomes a Waste Land, while the Guardian himself suffers from a Wound that will never heal until one comes who will break the enchantments and succeed in enduring the test of the Enchanted Games, in which a hero must face his own dark self in order to win the prize.

The search for the Court of the Rich Fisherman and its sacred treasure continues, though frustrated by the presence of a dark figure named Clingsor, who seeks the power of sovereignty, and of the mystical treasure for himself, and who founds the Order of the Peers of the Rich Menie in opposition to King Arthur's Fellowship of the Round Table. Meanwhile, in the forest, a child is born named Perceval, who is brought up in ignorance of the world, but whose destiny it is to be the one who will find the Court and release the imprisoned waters which will reawaken the soul of the land. But the youth receives bad advice from his mother and from an older man, and when he finds his way to the Court for the first time he fails to ask an all-important question concerning a strange procession which he sees pass before him, and which in fact consists of the very treasure for which he, and many others, are seeking. Because of this he has to wander again for many years, but he is helped by a hideous woman named Cundry who is herself a descendent of the Guardians of the Wells, and who has been called forth by the needs of the land itself. She is under a spell of enchantment, placed upon her by Clingsor, which maintains her ugly appearance until such time as she is able to discover a man who will not only agree to marry her, but who will give her the choice of how she will appear, fair or foul. Sir Gawain, King Arthur's nephew and representative, finally succeeds in achieving this test successfully, after himself wandering for many years in an unsuccessful quest for the Court of the Rich Fisherman.

Soon after this, Perceval returns to the Court and this time succeeds in facing the tasks set before him, which are to end the Enchanted Games and blow the horn which signifies the beginning of the restoration of the Court of the Rich Risherman, now called the Courts of Joy. Finally he asks the all-important question which sets in motion the healing of the Wounded King and the final restoration of the Land. With this the Guardians of the Wells return and the soul of the land is healed, ushering in a new period of freedom and joyfulness.

HEALING THE WOUNDED KING

Throughout this long journey through the country of the Grail you have met and worked with many different beings. You have sought healing for yourself and your environment through an interaction with the characters and situations in which the Quest Knights found their own way to the heart of the mystery. Yet at no point have you attempted to heal the Wounded King himself. It is time to redress this now, and to bring together the threads of your own journey in a final exercise in which you will have the opportunity to work both for yourself and the king.

Exercise 16 Healing the Wounded King

As you sink deeply into meditation you see before you a great wooden door made from massive, ancient timbers studded with iron nails. It opens at a touch and you go through, passing by way of a short, wide tunnel which issues onto open ground near the top of a hill. You step out and look around. Rolling downland sweeps away on all sides under a grey sky, and you feel the wind on your face. Before you a path leads downward into a shallow valley carpeted by a forest of ancient trees which stretches way into the distance. As you approach you see that the trees are tall and noble, looking as though they have stood there since the beginning of time. You pass beneath their branches and find yourself walking in a green and twilit world. The trees become denser the further you go, and a green canopy of leaves is over your head. Your feet make almost no sound on the thick carpet of leaves and moss which lines the forest floor.

Patches of sunlight fall slanting onto the pathway before you, and you find that you have come to a place where the way divides in three. A broad, well-trodden path leads away to the right, and a narrow, less frequented one to the left. Between these runs a twisting, winding path that leads deeper into the tangled heart of the wood. As you stand for a moment, hesitating over which path to take, you become aware of a single great tree, standing alone to one side of the twisting path. In its topmost branches sit two naked children, a boy and girl of about six or seven years, one dark, the other fair. As they look down at you from their perch they both seem sad, and as you look at them you are reminded of your own childhood, whether it is recent or in the more distant past. You spend a moment in contemplation of that time, and perhaps there comes to mind an old wound that began them. Give yourself a few moments to consider this and to be at peace with it . . . [Pause]

When you are done you see that the two children are both pointing silently to the narrow, twisting path, indicating that you should follow it deeper into the forest. You decide to take this road, and as you go on the air becomes still; there is an almost breathless feeling of expectation. Then the trees begin to open out ahead of you and you see that you are coming to a wide grassy glade. As you approach you become aware of a sound, high in the air above you. It is the sound of silvery bells, very faint and seeming far off. You are reminded of the bells worn by hunting hawks, which chime as they fly. As you emerge into the clearing you see that the branches of the encircling trees are hung with long palls of purple cloth, and that in the centre is a circle of tall, silvery birches, for all the world like the pillars of a great hall. At the centre of the clearing stands a great bed, draped in a hanging of red gold. On it lies a figure, wounded in many places from which blood runs down and soaks into the earth. The figure's eyes are closed as though in sleep, but it moves restlessly because of the pain of its wounds.

As you look at the wounded figure, you become aware of someone entering the clearing. You recognize him as your old friend the Hermit, with whom you have worked before. Smiling, he beckons you to follow him, and there at the edge of the clearing, almost hidden among the trees, is a low hut. The Hermit enters and comes forth again carrying a magnificent black cloak embroidered all over with golden doves. The Hermit looks directly at you, his eyes piercing your soul like a sword. 'Why are you here?' he asks. You look back towards the wounded figure and make it known that you have come to help in whatever way you can with the healing work that is required. The Hermit then hands the cloak to you and bids you put it on. The doves, he says, are the sign of the Grail. No harm can come to you as long as you go forward under their protection. Also he bids you listen for the chiming of the bells which you heard as you entered the clearing. They will help you if you encounter any difficulty on the way. Then he leads you back to the edge of the clearing furthest away from where you entered, and directs you to follow the path before you.

Soon you find yourself leaving the woodland and entering a misty part of the valley with high steep cliffs rising far off on either side. Ahead now you see a turbulent lake of water that boils and bubbles. Mists rise from its surface, making it impossible to see what lies beyond. Then you see that on the surface of the lake floats a small boat in which sits a man fishing. He seems unperturbed by the heat and mist rising from the water. Seeing you, he points to a spot further along the bank, where you catch a glimpse of a narrow bridge which stretches from the bank into the mist. It looks perilously narrow, without rope or rail on which to cling, but it is clear that you are meant to cross it.

You hesitate for a moment, remembering your previous attempts to cross the Sword Bridge, which in truth this resembles not a little, save that it seems even narrower and sharper than you remember. As you hesitate you become aware of a figure approaching along the margin of the lake. It is a woman, tall and graceful and dressed in black. You cannot see her face as she has both hands pressed to it, and you can hear that she is weeping bitterly. As she draws near you ask why she laments, and hear that it is because of the one who lies in the forest clearing, wounded unto death but unable to die or be healed. As long as this remains unchanged the crops will not grow and all the land is wasted.

As if scales had fallen from your eyes you look about you and see that the earth is barren on all sides of the valley. The grass grows sour and rank beneath your feet and the air is bitter with a tang like burning. You are filled with a great desire to heal this place, and turning again to the lady you see that her face is uncovered. She seems ugly to you, her face withered and marked with signs of weal and woe, and as you look at her you understand that if you are to heal the wounded one in the clearing you must cross the bridge and face whatever lies beyond. Remembering the words of the Hermit, that you are protected by the sign of the Grail, you draw your black and gold cloak around you and attempt the crossing . . .

You cross slowly, inching your way forward on hands and knees if need be. Feel the roughness of the stones beneath you, and hear the water bubbling below . . .

At last you feel firm earth beneath your feet again, and looking about you see that the mist is much thinner here. You are standing on what seems to be an island, which rises slightly towards the centre. There stands a tall white castle, which you have seen before in other journeys. This time, however, it is revolving . . . Time and again you see the gateway turn past you, and as there seems no other way of getting inside you are momentarily at a loss. Perhaps it is still not time for you to enter? But otherwise why would you have got this far? Thinking again of the wounded figure in the clearing, you hear the ringing of bells in the air above you, though you still cannot see from where they originate. Into your mind comes the thought that you must close your inner eyes and listen. Then, when you hear the bells again, you can go forward. In this way, you will be able to enter the castle, but you must trust yourself and your helpers, who are with you even though you do not always see them. . .

With inner eyes firmly closed you await the ringing of the bells, and when they sound you leap forward . . . to land safely on firm ground. You open your eyes to find that you are standing in a great hall, the walls of which seem made of glass, though you can see nothing beyond them since the mist has thickened around the castle. A weight of silence lies around you and there is scarcely a breath of air . . .

At the centre of the hall stands a great round table with chairs arranged about it. Standing to one side is the figure of the Hermit, who has somehow come there before you. He bids you welcome and invites you to sit at the table. As you approach you see that the chairs all have names inscribed on them, and that one of them bears your own name. On the others you see many names that you recognize, old friends and new, innerworld helpers and allies, teachers and people whom you have admired in your outer life . . .

A wonderful feast is laid before you by the servants of the place, and you will find that it consists of the food you like best. But this is spiritual food as well, that nourishes the soul as well as the body, and as you partake of the offering you feel new life and energy flowing though you . . .

Now become aware of a procession which passes through the hall. First comes a youth dressed in white and carrying a candlestick containing a candle that burns with a steady flame. Next comes a young woman who carries a tall spear. It seems as though it would be too heavy for her, yet she carries it easily. From its tip run shining drops of blood, which fall and are lost in shadow near the floor. Last of all comes a slightly older woman, fair of face, and crowned. In her hands she carries something covered in a white cloth. A soft radiance shines from within it, pulsing slowly like the beating of a great heart . . .

The procession slowly passes from view into a side chamber, and when it has gone the Hermit stands before you and bids you follow him. He leads you into the very same antechamber in which the procession went before you. Inside, the walls are surrounded by tall tree-like columns, so that you seem never to have left the clearing in the forest. In the middle of the room stands a wide bed, and in it lies the same wounded figure you saw earlier. Once again you hear the bells peal out above you . . .

Surrounding the bed are the people who passed you in the hall, and on a low stone altar the objects they carried are set out. The candle, burning still with a steady flame, stands to one side; the spear is laid slantwise across the altar; and the third object, now uncovered, stands in the centre. It appears to you as an ancient wooden Cup, blackened with age and cracked around the rim.

The Hermit indicates that you may, if you desire, take up the Cup and offer the wounded figure a drink. As you do this you should will with all your heart and mind and soul that the figure's wounds should heal. The Grail itself can do nothing unless it is charged with love and compassion. So now, in your own time, you may go forward and take up the Cup. The people of the procession will support the wounded one . . .

You go forward and lift the ancient Cup. A feeling of awe coupled with great strength flows through you as you bend over the wounded figure on the bed. Then you see, with wonder, and a sense of shock, that the wounded one is . . . yourself. You give yourself a drink from the ancient Cup, and will that with each sip, the wounds you possess will heal . . . [Pause]

When you have done what you came to do, the Hermit bids you once again to follow him back into the hall. As he does so he tells you that your work has been well done, and that the wounded figure has begun to recover. Now you must depart in the faith that the wounds will be completely healed.

The Hermit leads you back to the gate of the castle, which no longer revolves. As you depart you meet again the tall, graceful woman in black. But now she no longer weeps, and as you look into her face you see that she has lost the withered look she had before and now seems beautiful and radiant. She thanks you with these words: 'Now the Wounded One is almost healed, the land will bear fruit again.' She leads the way before you, and as you leave the island, crossing as you came by the slender bridge – which no longer seems to you at all unsafe – you see that the mists have lifted, and that it is dawn, and that on all sides are the first signs of a new spring: green buds bursting open on the trees and bushes, fresh green grass springing soft beneath your feet . . .

The dark queen leads the way back through the woods, and as you follow her you hear the sound of the bells once again high above you. Soon you find yourself again in the forest clearing, where the hangings are now all of gold and red, and where the wounded figure (who is also you) lies still on the great bed, but no longer seeming close to death. As you watch you see a hawk, the ringing of whose bells has guided so much of your journey, descend in a flash of brown and white feathers onto the body of the wounded one. But instead of tearing at the flesh, it merges with the body, and you understand at once that this is the soul of the wounded one – your own soul, returned to your body. Now the figure leaps up and embraces you – your true self embraces you – and thanks you for all you have done. The queen thanks you also and bids you remember all you have learned. You understand that in helping this wounded one to be healed not only have you brought healing to yourself, but given new strength to those who work constantly for the healing of the wounds of the world . . .

Now the Hermit comes forward and bids you keep the embroidered cloak in token of your Quest. It will be invisible to all but you, but as long as you possess it you may return at any time to the country of the Grail.

The Hermit sets you on the road home, and you walk back through the green woodlands where now birds sing joyfully amid the trees. On the way you pass again the great tree where the two children wave happily to you, all dark memories gone from them, as all are gone from you. And so you reach the green hillside and make your way up it until you see before you the great wooden door. It opens before you and you pass through, returning by way of the short passage to the place where you began this journey. Take time to re-establish contact with the outer world, and remember all that you experienced in the land of the Grail.

With this, the work of healing the Wounded King, who is yourself as he is everyone, is almost completed, and the Courts of Joy are restored within you. In time it will be fully accomplished. Now is the time to go back over any stages of the work which were, for whatever reason, left incomplete. And remember too that if the visualization above did not seem to be wholly successful, you can repeat it at any time. Once this work is concluded you will know that there is no need to return to the Grail Castle, except to visit those you have come to know so well.

It is important to understand, also, that only half the picture is represented by the words that make up this book. The rest must be completed by you, through the work you have accomplished by following the exercises. The insights and experience you have gained in this way are every bit as important as my words. You alone can complete the search for the Grail.

The mystery of our wounded nature is such that we can be both diminished by it and at the same time ennobled. The process of healing is such that it shows us how our wounds originated and what we can do to put them right. This is a simple enough truth, and once we are aware of it, it can lead us back onto the path to health and inner truth. The story of Perceval and the Wounded King tells us this in almost every line. Perceval's journey is from a state of woundedness to a state of well-being; on the way he heals others simply by being there. His journey is not easy – far from it – but when his wounded nature comes in contact with the wounded nature of others, an almost chemical reaction takes place at the soul level. The result is a great upsurge of well-being. Our fragmented souls are restored; we literally find the Courts of Joy through this experience. And, in doing so, we enter into a realm of fulfilment which separates us from our wounds and gives us the strength to deny them. Out of this, comes healing. Perceval sets free the waters, the Voices of the Wells are heard again, the Enchanted Games are ended. All this results from acknowledging the wounds within us, setting out to discover a cure, and finding the answer and uttering it *aloud* in the Courts of Joy. The Fisher King is the wounded part of ourselves, men and women alike. His wounds are our wounds; his healing is ours also. When we can recognize this, in our hearts and our souls, the Grail story will no longer be necessary – until we do, it remains one of the most powerful routes towards establishing wholeness.

In entering the enchanted realm of the Grail we have encountered many different forms of woundedness, and explored many different ways of finding healing. In the end, we are perhaps not unlike two young knights who once visited the castle of the Grail, long after it had fallen into disrepair and had almost been forgotten (as indeed it sometimes seems to be in the outer world today). They discovered something wonderful therein. The passage where this is described is a key one, and it seems a fitting place to end our journey together:

> The castle had been far from any people and look . . . but no one . . . dared go there, save two . . . knights who had heard about it; they were . . . very young and high-spirited, and they swore to each other than they would go, and full of excitement they entered the castle. They stayed there for a long while . . . It was a hard life, but it pleased them greatly, and when people asked them why they were living thus, they would reply: 'Go where we went, and you will know why.'(15)

If there is one thing that the story of the Wounded King teaches us, it is how to live life in a different way: to see everything with new eyes, to handle the adventures that come our way with a lighter touch. Nothing may seem to change; but *everything* will change, and the world will become a very different place. And, in time, you will be able to say, like those young knights who went to the ruined castle where the Grail once was – or is still – Go where we went, and you will know why!

Appendix 1

There are many characters, some more important than others, in the story of the Grail and the Wounded King. Many will be unfamiliar to those who have never encountered the Arthurian mythos. The following list includes all the main characters in the stories which are explored in this book, as well as one or two related characters from Celtic tradition. They appear under their given names (where this is known). Where no such name exists, or where the title by which they are known is more familiar (for example the **Grail Maiden** appears under this title rather than by the name **Elaine**) this is given precedence. A brief account of the history of their wounds or their function in the story is also given.

Amangons   King who is the supposed protector of the **Damsels of the Wells**. Desiring one of them, he rapes her and steals the golden cup with which she is wont to offer succour to weary travellers. When they see this, Amangons' men follow suit with other of the Damsels, thus creating an area of desolation known as the **Waste Land**. He is one of the **Anti-Grail Kings.**

Anti-Grail Kings Characters who appear in the various stories as opposing or negative aspects of the Grail Kings, and who seek to use the healing power of the Grail for their own ends. The names of the best known are **Amangons, Garlon** and **Clingsor**.

Balin Le Sauvage A knight of Arthur's court who strikes the Dolorous Blow and causes the wounding of the Grail King Pellam. Balin first slays the evil **Garlon,** then fleeing in fear snatches up the sacred Grail Spear and inflicts Pellam with a wound in the thighs. Balin subsequently dies in a fratricidal conflict with his own brother. Balin's wounds manifest through his aggressive character, which causes him to act without thought and often in a violent manner.

Clingsor An evil magician who desires the Grail to enhance his own power. Learning of the wound suffered by the Grail King he castrates himself in an attempt to receive what he perceives as the benefits of the Wound. He typifies all those who try to use their wounded state to gain power and authority over others.

Courts of Joy Sometimes known as the Court of the Rich Fisherman, they are a metaphor for the outburst of joy at the healing of the **Wounded King** and the **Waste Land.**

Cundry Also known as the **Hideous Maiden,** she is a darkly ugly woman who appears during the Quest and berates the unsuccessful hero for not having asked the question. She also offers help and advice to those who would continue the search. Her primary role in the story is to represent the wounded earth of the **Waste Lands,** whose voice she is, and which has, in some way, called her into being.

Damsels of the Wells Guardians of sacred wells scattered throughout the land of Logres (Arthur's Britain). The Maidens serve all travellers who come their way, and speak with the Voices of the Wells until **Amangons** and his followers rape them and steal their golden cups. The result is the Waste Land, a sterile and wounded area around the Castle of the Grail, and the loss of the Voices of the Land and access to the **Court of the Rich Fisherman**. In terms of the **Wounded King** mythos they represent the wounded feminine.

Dindraine The sister of **Perceval**. She is brought up in a monastery and at an early age decides to follow the path of an anchoress, living a solitary life in a tiny cell in the forest. There she receives a vision of the Grail and sets forth on her own quest. Later she joins with Perceval and Galahad, and on arriving at a castle where a woman is sick with leprosy gives her blood to heal the woman and dies as a result. Her body is placed in a magical vessel and reaches the sacred city of the Grail before any of her companions. Her wounds are a triumphal reversal of the negative aspect of woundedness, and she represents a powerful route to healing through unselfish love and spiritual vision.

Enchanted Games Founded by **Erec**, these are really Sovereignty's Games, in which the hero is required to do battle with his own dark self in the shape of Mabonagrain the Black Knight, and on winning, sound the note of joy which signals both the end of the games and the restoration of the **Courts of Joy**.

Erec/Geraint Originally a Celtic hero, Erec is one of the premier knights of Arthur's Round Table. After a misunderstanding with his wife Enide he forces her to ride in front of him, wearing the same dress and keeping silence in the face of all eventualities. After many adventures Erec succeeds in ending the **Enchanted Games,** and wins back the love and affection of his wife. His wounds assert themselves through his impetuosity and thoughtlessness, and his inability to understand the actions of others.

Garlon Brother to Pellam the Grail King, he is given to striking down his opponents while wearing a cloak of invisibility. He thus represents the shadow side of the Wounded King. He is slain by **Balin**, but his death ultimately is one of the causes of the Waste Land and the wounding of his brother.

Grail The sacred vessel sought by the Knights of the Round Table. It provides healing and sustenance to those who come within its presence. In some texts it is associated with the Cauldron of Celtic tradition, in others with the Cup of the Last Supper.

Grail Maiden/Princess Sometimes known as Elaine the White. She carries the Grail in the mysterious procession which passes through the hall of the Grail Castle to be witnessed by the hero. In the later versions of the story she is the mother of Galahad, the successful Grail winner who supersedes **Perceval**.

Her wound derives from her inability to act and to heal her own father.

Hermit   Brother to the **Wounded King, Garlon** and Perceval's mother, he is a saintly man whose part in the Grail Quest is to act as advisor, confessor and guide to those who are seeking the miraculous vessel.

Mabon   The Celtic god of youth and inspiration, who is imprisoned before he is two nights old, and only rescued many years later by the hero Culhwch, assisted by the Warriors of Arthur. He appears in the Arthurian mythos as Mabonagrain, the champion of the Enchanted Games. In terms of the inner mythology of the Wounded King he represents the wounds of youth, and the loss of the bright energy of childhood.

Perceval   The archetypal hero of the Grail story. He grows up in isolation in the Waste Forest and is drawn to Arthur's court after meeting with some knights. A simple and uncomplicated youth, he follows the advice of his mother and his knightly mentor so closely that he fails to ask the all-important question concerning the Grail and the Spear, and is forced to wander the ways again until he finds his way back to the Grail Castle. This time he succeeds in bringing healing to the **Wounded King**. His role in the mythos of woundedness is to represent all those who seek to heal, but who are themselves wounded. He thus equates to the wounded shamanic healers who travel into the Otherworld to bring back lost soul-parts on behalf of their wounded clients. Perceval is wounded by his mother's over-protective immuring of him in the forest.

Ragnall   Also known as the Loathly Damsel, she is both a representative of Sovereignty, of wounded or calumniated womanhood, and of the Hideous Damsel, whose task it is to test those who go in search of the Grail, and to encourage them to follow the right path. In the stories she marries Sir Gawain, and through him receives back her right to beauty.

Waste Land   An area of ruined and infertile land around the Grail Castle, brought about as the result of the wounding of the King, whose symbiotic relationship with the land means that if he is sick the earth is sick also. It can only be restored when the

Wounded King is healed and the waters of life are allowed to flow again.

Wounded King Sometimes known by the name Pellam, at other as Amfortas. The guardian of the Grail who possesses an un-healing wound which can only be healed when the right person asks a ritual question concerning the mysterious Grail Procession. In terms of the biography of healing he represents everyone, both men and women, who suffer from wounds of the spirit and the soul which will not heal.

Widow of the Waste Forest The mother of **Perceval**, who brings her son up in ignorance of knightly pursuits after her husband and older sons are killed in battle. She lives an utterly withdrawn life and dies soon after Perceval leaves her. Her wounds are those of grief and fear, which cause her to act in an inappropriate manner and to force her youngest child into a mould for which he was never intended.

Appendix 2

This list of questions grew out of the workshops I taught on the subject between 1993 and 1995, and was subsequently sent out to various people around the world. It is included here, in a slightly edited form, in the hope that it might help readers in focusing their own questions concerning woundedness.

1 Which of the two main stories, 'The Wounded King' or 'The Voices of the Wells', had the deepest effect upon you?
2 What is the 'Grail' to you?
3 Why do you think the King was wounded?
4 Whose fault was it – or should one not attach blame?
5 In the story of the Wells is the result of Amangons' action positive or negative?
6 How would you define the inner relationship between Garlon and the Fisher King, and between Amangons and Arthur?
7 What do you think is meant by the 'Voices of the Wells'?
8 What wounds are you aware of in yourself?
9 How do you think the stories relate to your own sense of woundedness?
10 What do you feel are the principle causes of woundedness in men and women?
11 Would you look for the principle causes of woundedness in: a) childhood b) adolescence c) adulthood d) all three?
12 How would you go about seeking healing in the terms of the Wounded King story?
13 In the stories, whom did you identify with most strongly?
14 What are The Courts of Joy for you?

Resources

A number of tapes are available to accompany shamanic journey work. Some of these are produced by the author and may be obtained from the address below. In addition, John and Caitlín Matthews offer courses in shamanism and related subjects. Details of this and news of publications are included in the quarterly *Hallowquest Newsletter*, which can be obtained by sending a stamped addressed envelope and eight first-class stamps (UK) or US$5 (worldwide) for a sample issue to: BCM Hallowquest, London, WC1N 3XX.

TAPES

Celtic Shamanism Journeys, visualization, singing and chants to extend practical work in Celtic shamanism.

Just Drumming Four 20-minute drumming tracks to accompany the shamanic journey.

Shamanizing Drumming, chants and journeys to accompany the book *The Celtic Shaman* by John Matthews.

Silver Branch Journeys Visualizations on Celtic Otherworld Themes by Caitlín Matthews.

Soul Flights Four tracks for shamanic journey work with drum and gong by Caitlín Matthews.

The Wounded King Designed to accompany this book, it includes all the visualizations read by the author. (Available shortly: please write to the above address for further details.)

Further Reading

Texts

The literature of the Grail is vast. Here are just a few of the most important texts which should be read by all those involved in the Quest for healing. The numbers before each title correspond to references within the text.

1 *Ancient Irish Tales* Trans T P Cross & C H Slover, Figgis, Dublin, 1936
2 *Didot Perceval* Trans Dell Skeeles, Washington University Press, 1966
3 *Diu Crone (The Crown)* Heinrich von dem Tulin, trans J W Thomas, Nebraska University Press, 1989
4 *Early Irish Myths and Sagas* Trans J Gantz, Penguin Books, Harmondsworth, 1981
5 *The Elucidation* Ed A W Thompson, Publications of the Institute of French Studies, 1931
6 *The Elucidation* Trans Sebastian Evans, *In Quest of the Holy Grail*, J M Dent, London, 1898
7 *Erec and Enide* Chretien de Troyes, ed & trans C W Carroll (in) *Arthurian Romances*, Penguin Books, Harmondsworth, 1991
8 *Four Ancient Books of Wales* Ed & trans W W Skeat, AMS Press, 1992
9 *Lancelot-Grail* General ed Norris J Lacy, Garland Publishing, 1993–96 (5 vols)
10 *The Mabinogion* Trans by J Gantz, Penguin Books, Harmondsworth, 1976
11 *The Mabinogion* Trans Lady Charlotte Guest, J M Dent, London, 1906
12 *Le Morte Darthur* Sir Thomas Malory, University Books, 1966
13 *Parzival* Wolfram von Eschenbach, trans A T Hatto, Penguin Books, Harmondsworth, 1980
14 *Perceval, (The Story of the Grail)* Chretien de Troyes, trans N Bryant, Boydell & Brewer, Suffolk, 1976

15 *Perlesvaus (The High Book of the Grail)* Trans N Bryant, Boydell & Brewer, Suffolk, 1978

16 *Sir Gawain at the Grail Castle* (including texts from the 3rd continuation), trans J L Weston, D Nutt, 1903

17 *The Wedding of Sir Gawain and Dame Ragnell A Modern Spelling Edition of a Middle English Romance* John Withrington, Department of English, Lancaster University, 1991

General Works

There are a number of important books concerned with the Grail and its work in the world that helped in the development of this book. Here is just a selection of the many titles available.

18 Bly, Robert, *Iron John*, Element Books, Shaftesbury, Dorset, 1991

19 Brown, Norman O, *Life Against Death*, Welshyan UP, Middleton, Conn, 1970

20 Eisner, S, *A Tale of Wonder*, John English, Wexford, 1957

21 Fleischer, Leonore, *The Fisher King: A novel based on the motion picture by Richard La Gravenese*, Penguin Books, London, 1991

22 Ingerman, Sandra, 'The Shamanic Journey: A Way to Retrieve Our Souls' in *Nourishing the Soul*, ed A & C Simpkinson and R Solari, Harper Collins, New York, 1995

23 Ingerman, Sandra, *Soul Retrieval: Mending the Fragmented Self*, Harper Collins, New York, 1993

24 Johnson, Kenneth and Marguerite Elsbeth, *The Grail Castle: Male Myths and Mysteries in the Celtic Tradition*, Llewellyn Publications, St Paul Mn, 1995

25 Johnson, Robert A, *The Fisher King and the Handless Maiden*, Harper San Francisco, New York, 1993

26 Johnson, Robert A, *He: Understanding Masculine Psychology*, Harper and Row, New York and London, 1989

27 Johnson, Robert A, 'Learning to Serve the Soul' in *Nourishing the Soul*, ed A Simpkinson & R Solari, Harper Collins, San Francisco, 1995

28 Jung, Emma & von Franz, Marie-Louise, *The Grail Legend*, Hodder & Stoughton, London, 1970

29 Lawlor, Robert, *Earth Honouring: The New Male Sexuality*, Park Street Press, Vermont, 1969

30 Matthews, Caitlín, *Arthur and the Sovereignty of Britain*, Arkana, London, 1989

31 Matthews, Caitlín, *Mabon and the Mysteries of Britain*, Arkana, London, 1988

32 Matthews, Caitlín, *Singing the Soul Back Home*, Element Books, Shaftesbury, Dorset, 1995

33 Matthews, Caitlín, *In Search of Woman's Passionate Soul: Revealing the Daimon Lover Within*, Element Books, Shaftesbury, Dorset, 1997

34 Matthews, Caitlín & John, *Ladies of the Lake*, Aquarian Press, London, 1992
35 Matthews, John, *The Arthurian Tradition*, Element Books, Shaftesbury, Dorset, 1995
36 Matthews, John, *The Celtic Shaman*, Element Books, Shaftesbury, Dorset, 1994
37 Matthews, John (with Chesca Potter), *The Celtic Shaman's Pack*, Element Books, Shaftesbury, Dorset, 1995
38 Matthews, John, *Gawain, Knight of the Goddess*, Thorsons, London, 1991
39 Matthews, John, *King Arthur & the Grail Quest*, Blandford Press, London, 1995
40 Matthews, John, *Taliesin: Shamanism & the Bardic Mysteries in Britain & Ireland*, Harper Collins, London, 1991
41 Matthews, John (ed), *The Household of the Grail*, Thorsons, London, 1990
42 Matthews, John (ed), *Sources of the Grail: A Collection of Writings*, Floris Books, Edinburgh, 1996
43 Matthews, John & Green, Marian, *The Grail Seeker's Companion*, Thorsons, London, 1986
44 Moore, Thomas, *Care of the Soul*, Harper Collins, London & New York, 1992
45 Moore, Thomas, *Soul Mates: Honouring the Mysteries of Love and Relationship*, Element Books, Shaftesbury, Dorset, 1994
46 Myss, Caroline, *Why People Don't Heal* (audio tapes), Sounds True Recordings, Boulder, Colorado, 1995
47 Nagy, Joseph Falaky, *The Wisdom of the Outlaw: the Boyhood Deeds of Finn in Gaelic Narrative Tradition*, University of California Press, Berkley, California, 1985
48 Nelson, Gertrude Mueller, *Here All Dwell Free: Stories to Heal the Wounded Feminine*, Doubleday, New York & London, 1991
49 Peate, F David, *Blackfoot Physics*, Fourth Estate, London, 1996
50 Sardello, Robert, *Facing the World With Soul: The Reimagination of Modern Life*, Lindisfarne Press, New York, 1992
51 Sardello, Robert, *Love and the Soul: Creating a Future for Earth*, Harper Collins, London & New York, 1995
52 Simpkinson, Anne & Charles and Solari, Rose, (eds), *Nourishing the Soul*, Harper Collins, New York, 1995
53 Stone, Alby, *The Bleeding Lance: Myth, Ritual and the Grail Legend*, Heart of Albion Press, Loughborough, 1992
54 Stone, Alby, 'Bran, Odin, and the Fisher King: Norse Tradition and the Grail Legends' in *Folk-Lore*, vol 100 No 1 (1989) pp 106–15
55 Stone, Alby, 'The Perilous Bridge' in *At the Edge*, No 1, March 1996, pp 7–10
56 Sussman, Linda, *The Speech of the Grail*, Lindisfarne Press, New York, 1995
57 Weston, Jessie L, *From Ritual to Romance*, Doubleday Anchor Books, New York, 1957
58 Weston, Jessie L 'The Grail and the Rites of Adonis' in *Sources of the Grail*, ed by J Matthews, Floris Books, Edinburgh, 1996

59 Whitmont, Edward, *Return of the Goddess: Femininity, Aggression and the Modern Grail Quest*, Routledge & Kegan Paul, London, 1983

60 Wieland, Friedmann, *The Journey of the Hero*, Dorset, Prism Press, Bridport, 1991

61 Woodman, Marion, *The Ravaged Bridegroom: Masculinity in Women*, Inner City Books, Toronto, 1990

62 Woolger, Roger J, 'The Holy Grail: Healing the Sexual Wound in the Western Psyche' in *Pilgrimage* Vol II, No 2, Summer 1983

63 Young-Eisendrath, Polly, *Hags and Heroes: A Feminist Approach to Jungian Psychotherapy with Couples*, Inner City Books, Toronto, 1984

Index